Mysterious You

Zzz....

The most interesting book you'll ever read about sleep

Written by Trudee Romanek

Illustrated by Rose Cowles

Kids Can Press

Tremendous thanks are due to Dr. James MacFarlane of the Centre for Sleep and Chronobiology in Toronto for his invaluable review of this book. Thanks also to Dr. Claudio Stampi, director of Boston's Chronobiology Research Institute, Dr. J. J. Lipsitz and the Sleep Disorders Centre of Metropolitan Toronto, and the many sleep scientists who have given up countless nights of sleep in the name of research. And finally, I am grateful to editors Linda Biesenthal and Val Wyatt for their patience and guidance, and to Rose Cowles, whose artwork truly brings a book to life.

Kids Can Press acknowledges the financial support of the Ontario Arts Council, the Canada Council for the Arts and the Government of Canada, through the BPIDP, for our publishing activity.

Published in Canada by
Kids Can Press Ltd.
29 Birch Avenue
Toronto, ON M4V 1E2

Published in the U.S. by
Kids Can Press Ltd.
2250 Military Road
Tonawanda, NY 14150

www.kidscanpress.com

Edited by Linda Biesenthal and Valerie Wyatt
Designed by Marie Bartholomew
Printed in Hong Kong by Wing King Tong Company Limited

The hardcover edition of this book is smyth sewn casebound.
The paperback edition of this book is limp sewn with a drawn-on cover.

CM 02 0 9 8 7 6 5 4 3 2 1
CM PA 02 0 9 8 7 6 5 4 3 2 1

National Library of Canada Cataloguing in Publication Data

Romanek, Trudee
   Zzz...: the most interesting book you'll ever read about sleep

(Mysterious you)
Includes index.

ISBN 1-55074-944-7 (bound)   ISBN 1-55074-946-3 (pbk.)

1. Sleep — Juvenile literature. I. Cowles, Rose, 1967– II. Title.
III. Series: Mysterious you (Toronto, Ont.)

QP425.R64 2002   j612.8'21   C2001-901747-2

Kids Can Press is a Nelvana company

Contents

Sleep for Life

It's 3 A.M. on May 20, 1927, and Charles Lindbergh can't sleep. In a few hours, the daring pilot will take off from New York, hoping to become the first person to fly solo across the Atlantic Ocean. But without a good night's sleep, will he be able to stay alert during the 30-hour flight to Paris?

When his plane takes off just before 8 A.M., Lindbergh has had no sleep for 24 hours. As night falls, he struggles to stay awake and has to use his fingers to hold his eyes open. After 50 hours without sleep, even the thrill of the flight can't keep Lindbergh awake. He nods off and his plane flies out of control. Suddenly, the pilot wakes — just in time to avoid crashing into the ocean. Almost 60 hours since he last slept, Lindbergh spots the Paris airfield and prepares to land.

Lindbergh was lucky to make it safely to Paris. Like you, even famous pilots need sleep. Sleep gives your body a chance to grow and repair itself, and it keeps your brain alert so you can think straight. Sleep is one of life's necessities — you can't survive without it.

- Weightlifters who were allowed only three hours of sleep one night couldn't lift as much weight the next day.

- When your body is trying to heal itself, your cells release a substance to make you sleepy. Even recovering from a sunburn can make you sleep more.

- Tests show that when a person stays up until 3 A.M., the next day their body has 30 percent fewer "natural killer cells" — the cells that fight viruses.

Losing Sleep

Strange things start to happen when you don't get the sleep you need. Losing just two hours sleep in one night can affect how alert you are and how well you do things the next day. After one full night without sleep, you might have a hard time choosing the right words when you speak. You'd begin to feel worried and depressed. Your judgment and ability to make decisions wouldn't be as good. Your memory would begin to fail, and you'd have a hard time concentrating. You'd take twice as long as usual to react to things, and your body would have difficulty fighting off infections. Whew! And all because you missed just one night's sleep.

Super Sleeper

Ever heard the story of Rip Van Winkle? One evening while hunting, Rip lay down and fell asleep. He awoke to find his rifle covered in rust and his chin covered in a long beard. It turns out he'd been asleep for 20 years. Believe it or not, you will sleep for 20 years, too — just not all at once!

Sleep is so important that we spend a third of each day doing it. That's almost 3000 hours, or more than four months, each year. And that means if you live to be 70 years old, you'll spend about 23 years sleeping — more than Rip Van Winkle himself.

Are You Sleeping?

In 1976, researchers at Stanford University allowed a volunteer to sleep just four hours one night. The next day, they asked him to lie on a bed with his eyes taped open. They placed a bright light just 15 cm (6 in.) above his face and flashed it every few seconds. The volunteer was to tap a switch whenever he saw the light flash. For several minutes, he tapped the switch after each flash. Then, after one flash, he did nothing. When the researchers asked him why he hadn't tapped the switch, the volunteer said the light had not flashed. The man had become so tired that, without realizing it, he simply fell asleep for a few seconds with his eyes open.

When you're awake, you notice things around you because your brain is responding to messages from your senses. You hear the radio playing, smell dinner cooking, feel cool air on your skin. And you remember most things that happen. Being asleep is a different story. Think about it. Do you remember if it rained last night, or how many times you rolled over in your sleep? Probably not. When you're sleeping, your brain doesn't react to all the messages from your senses, and you're not nearly as aware of what's happening around you.

Red Alert!!

You're sound asleep when suddenly a screeching sound jolts you wide awake. It's the smoke alarm. But if your brain isn't aware of things around you as you sleep, how did the noise wake you? Although you may not remember hearing other, quieter sounds, your ears did sense them. It's just that the messages your ears sent reached only part of your brain. That part decided the sound wasn't important enough to interrupt your sleep. Loud sounds that could mean danger, however, usually get your whole brain's attention and wake you up.

• On May 17, 1928, Alvin "Shipwreck" Kelly climbed to a platform the size of a dinner plate at the top of a flagpole in Louisville, Kentucky. He was determined to perch there for 100 hours. Doctors warned that he would drift off to sleep and fall, but somehow Alvin managed to last for a full four days and eight hours.

You Try It

Remember the fairy-tale princess who slept poorly because of a pea under her mattress? Like the princess, most sleepers react to things that bother them while they sleep. Ask your brother (or someone else) if you can try these tests on him 15 minutes after he falls asleep. Or have him try them on you.

• Gently place a tennis ball under his back. He will likely change position without waking up. That's because the uncomfortable pressure of the ball sends a message to part of his brain without waking the rest of it.

• Gently touch his face with a feather or piece of string. Did he try to brush it away without rousing from sleep?

Feeling Sleepy?

It's been a busy day. An hour before bedtime, you start feeling sleepy and begin to yawn. Your temperature drops a few tenths of a degree. Your body is gearing down for its nightly rest.

Once in bed, you relax. You may feel as though you are falling, or your body may suddenly jerk. You may "see" things that aren't there and hear voices. These are hypnagogic (hip-nuh-GAW-jik) hallucinations. They occur as you cross the line between wakefulness and sleep. Then after about 20 minutes — click! You enter the mysterious land of sleep.

Inside the Sleeping Brain

Once you're asleep, your brain stem — the part that looks after your body's automatic systems — slows down your breathing, heart rate, digestion and urine production. But the brain itself changes when you're sleeping, too.

Your brain produces different kinds of electrical activity — called "brainwaves" — depending on what you're doing. Your "asleep" brainwaves are different from those your brain produces when you're awake.

Experts can tell the moment a person falls asleep just by looking at the changes in the pattern of the brainwaves recorded by a machine called an electroencephalograph (EEG). Take a look at the brainwave recording below. The red circle marks the point when this person fell asleep.

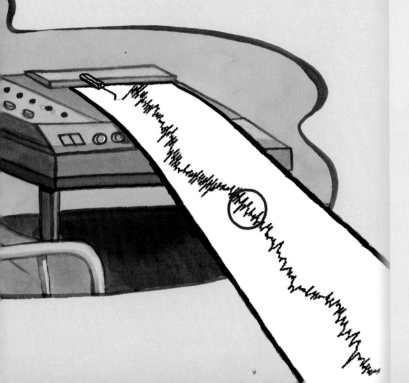

Yawn!

Like a sneeze, a yawn happens whether you want it to or not. A yawn makes you open your mouth wide and take a slow, deep breath. Your lungs expand with air, and your jaw muscles stretch to hold your mouth open for about six seconds.

The deep breath sends more oxygen to your body and especially to your brain. It also helps clear out carbon dioxide, the gas we breathe out. That may be why you yawn, although scientists aren't quite sure.

Mostly, people yawn just before bed or when they wake up, but just thinking about yawning can make you yawn. You may even be yawning while you're reading this! And when one person yawns, people nearby may yawn, too. Try yawning a few times during dinner. Did you get anyone else at the table yawning?

The Body's Clock

Ever wondered what makes you sleepy at bedtime? Is it just that you're tired out from a long day? That may be part of it, but you also get tired because your brain tells you to. A tiny part of each person's brain controls at what time of the day you'll feel wide awake and what time you'll feel sleepy.

People call this part of the brain the biological clock, or the body clock. Of course, it's not really a clock. It's actually two tiny clumps of nerve cells — about the size of two pinheads — inside your brain. The real name of these clumps of cells is the suprachiasmatic nuclei (SOO-pra-ki-az-MAT-ik NOO-klee-i), or the SCN for short. They help your brain produce the right chemicals, called neurotransmitters and hormones, to make you feel sleepy as bedtime gets nearer and ready to rise as morning approaches.

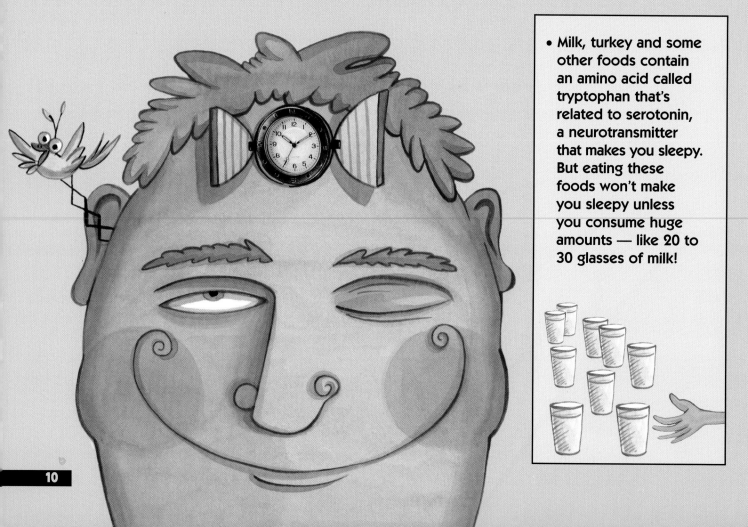

- Milk, turkey and some other foods contain an amino acid called tryptophan that's related to serotonin, a neurotransmitter that makes you sleepy. But eating these foods won't make you sleepy unless you consume huge amounts — like 20 to 30 glasses of milk!

Putting the Brain to Sleep

During the day, your biological clock triggers your body to produce chemicals that stimulate your brain and keep it alert. While it's alert, a part of your brain stem — the lower part of your brain that looks after breathing and other basic life functions — is hard at work. It passes information non-stop from your senses to your cerebral cortex — the upper part of your brain that sorts out information from your senses and controls speech and all your other muscle movements.

Later, your biological clock signals your body that bedtime is approaching. When the daylight begins to fade, your pineal gland churns out more melatonin, a hormone that lets your organs know it's time for sleep. Your brain starts producing less of the stimulating, wake-up chemicals. Eventually, another part of the brain stem (the pontine nuclei) takes over, allowing you to sleep. Once this part is in charge, very little sensory information is passed to your cerebral cortex and you are no longer as aware of things around you.

The brain stem itself doesn't seem to need sleep. It may be the part of your brain that stays alert during sleep, waiting for important signals.

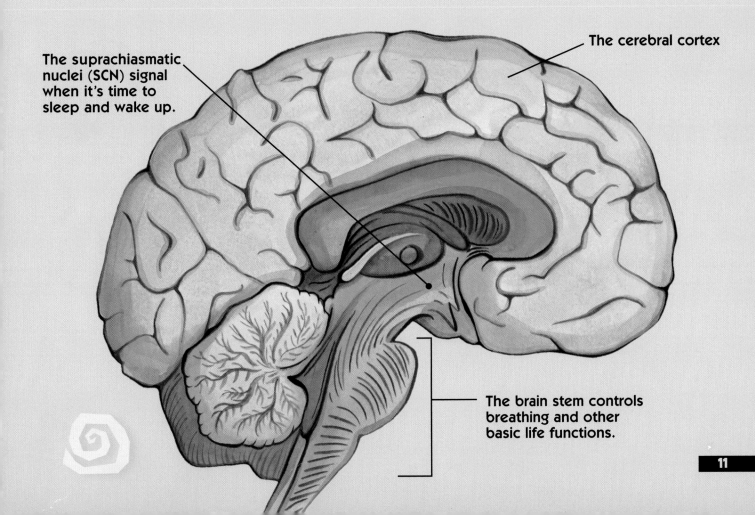

The suprachiasmatic nuclei (SCN) signal when it's time to sleep and wake up.

The cerebral cortex

The brain stem controls breathing and other basic life functions.

Right On Time

People are creatures of habit, thanks in part to their biological clocks. Scientists have discovered that, over the course of each day, human beings (and other animals, too) have a distinct pattern of times when they are sleepy and times when they are alert. Most people feel energetic in the morning, then start to feel sleepy after lunch. They perk up in late afternoon, feel wide awake right after supper and then get tired at bedtime. This sleep/wake cycle is part of a larger, 24-hour pattern called the circadian rhythm.

Some other events in your day are part of your circadian rhythm as well. For example, your body temperature rises just before you wake up and falls during the night. And your stomach produces digestive juices according to a schedule, so that at meal times it's ready to break down the food you eat.

9–11 A.M.

1–4 P.M.

6–8 P.M.

Gathering Evidence

Your biological clock uses a number of different clues to make sure it's keeping your circadian rhythm on schedule. Eating and exercising at regular times, even brushing your teeth and putting on your pajamas before bed can signal your brain that everything is happening when it's supposed to. But the most important time clue for your biological clock is daylight.

When your eyes sense light, optical fibers carry the message to your brain and your SCN. As long as your eyes are sensing bright light during the day and no light at night, your biological clock knows that it's waking you up, making you sleepy and triggering all those other events at the correct times.

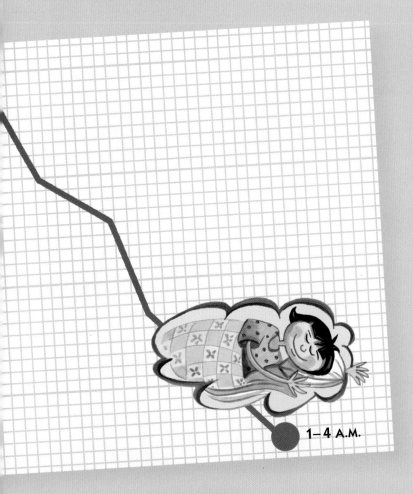

1–4 A.M.

Flowers that Tell Time

Researchers have found that almost every living thing — animals, insects and even bacteria and fungi — has a biological clock that structures its day and night. Bees, for example, only gather nectar from flowers at a certain time of the day. Even plants often have a daily schedule.

In 1748, a Swedish scientist named Carolus Linnaeus planted a sort of garden clock. Each kind of plant in his garden opened or closed its flowers at a different, specific time of day. Linnaeus could tell what time it was just by looking at which flowers were open.

Turning Day into Night

Many animals, including humans, are diurnal — awake and active during the day. These days, though, many businesses are open 24 hours. Employees on night shift have to sleep during the day instead. This can cause big problems.

If you switched night for day and day for night long enough, your body might get used to the change. The problem is that most shiftworkers don't stick to the new schedule for long, so their bodies don't have time to adjust. As a result shiftworkers often feel sleepy at work, but lie awake in bed when they're supposed to be sleeping.

Sleepy Heads

Air traffic controllers at a Los Angeles airport were surprised when the crew of an approaching jet didn't answer their radio calls. Then, instead of turning to land, the jet continued straight toward the Pacific Ocean. The reason? It was flying on autopilot because the entire flight crew had fallen asleep! The jet flew 165 km (100 mi.) off course before someone in the control tower set off an alarm in the cockpit and woke the crew.

Flying from one time zone to another can throw your body into a tailspin. Suddenly the hours between sunrise and sunset don't add up to a complete day. The more time zones you cross, the more out of whack your biological clock gets. Your brain may produce chemicals that keep you wide awake when everyone else is asleep. It can take a week before daylight resets your clock and gets all the systems of your circadian rhythm back to normal.

- In space, astronauts sometimes face their most difficult tasks when they would normally be sleeping back on Earth. So, before a mission, NASA shines bright lights on the astronauts in the middle of the night to reset their biological clocks.

Getting off Schedule

Many teenagers have a problem called teenage phase shift. Even though their bodies are growing a lot, they don't produce more melatonin — the chemical that signals it's time for bed. So the melatonin signal is weaker, and they don't feel sleepy until well after midnight. Getting up is a nightmare, and they drag themselves around exhausted for the rest of the day. By evening, they're wide awake again and can't get to sleep. To deal with the problem of sleepy teens, some U.S. high schools are starting classes later in the morning so that students can get the sleep they need.

Stages of Sleep

In 1952, American researcher Nathaniel Kleitman began studying the eyes of sleepers. He knew that our eyes roll around slowly just as we're falling asleep. But he didn't know if this happened at other times during the night as well.

Kleitman asked a research student, Eugene Aserinsky, to stay awake all night and watch a sleeping person's eyes. Aserinsky was astonished by what he saw. Although the sleeper's eyeballs didn't roll, from time to time they darted very quickly back and forth under closed eyelids. What Kleitman and Aserinsky had discovered was a special stage of sleep. They named it Rapid Eye Movement (REM) sleep and soon found that it's during REM sleep that sleepers have their most elaborate dreams.

Sleep researchers everywhere began to monitor brainwaves throughout the whole night. What they found was that the brainwaves changed during the night, not just once, but many times. They divided the different types of brainwaves into five stages of sleep that people go through each night — REM sleep and stages 1, 2, 3 and 4 of non-REM sleep.

- Almost all mammals have periods of light and deep sleep and periods of REM sleep, but researchers can't detect the two clear patterns of REM and non-REM sleep in reptiles.

Non-REM Sleep

Stage 1 sleep is so close to being awake that if you were woken from it you'd probably say you weren't even asleep. After several minutes in Stage 1, you sink into Stage 2 sleep. The brainwaves during this stage are a little larger and slower than at Stage 1. From there you sink into the deeper sleep of Stages 3 and 4. Your body is very relaxed and it is difficult to wake you. During Stage 4, your body produces the largest amount of some of the chemicals that help you grow.

Stages 1 and 2 are often called light sleep. Stages 3 and 4 are called deep sleep, or Slow-Wave Sleep (SWS), because your brainwaves are larger and slower in those stages.

Asleep in the Snow?

If you think hibernating animals just snooze through the winter, think again. When scientists monitored the brainwaves of some hibernators, they discovered that the animals didn't produce any brainwaves at all for most of the time. Every few weeks, though, the brainwave monitoring showed that the animals did drift up from hibernation into sleep for a couple of hours before sinking back into a hibernation state again.

Most experts think that animals hibernate to slow their bodies' systems so that they can survive with less food during the snowy season when there is less to eat.

The Sleep Cycle

Throughout the night, you make your way through the five stages of sleep on a very regular schedule. After falling asleep, you drift down through light sleep (Stages 1 and 2) and then into deep SWS sleep (Stages 3 and 4). You stay in Stage 4 sleep for about 20 minutes, your longest chunk of it for the night. Then, you begin to drift back up through Stage 3 and into the lighter sleep of Stage 2. But instead of passing into Stage 1 and then waking up, you enter your first period of REM (rapid eye movement) sleep.

For the rest of the night you pass up and down through the stages of sleep in cycles that last a little more than an hour. You spend less time in deep SWS and more time in REM sleep as the night passes. In fact, most people have no deep sleep at all after about 2 A.M.

• Most small mammals have shorter sleep cycles than larger mammals. A mouse passes through its sleep cycle in nine minutes, an elephant takes as long as two hours.

Sleeping like a Baby

Newborn babies don't seem to have much of a sleep cycle. They sleep for an hour or two, wake up for a while and then fall asleep again — no matter what time of day it is. Even though they sleep so much, most babies don't get any deep sleep (Stage 3 or 4) at all until they're about three months old. Instead, they spend half of their sleep time in Stages 1 and 2 of light sleep and the other half — around eight hours each day — in REM sleep. Babies get this large amount of REM sleep at the time their brains are developing the most. Some scientists think REM sleep somehow helps the brain develop. By the age of three, children spend only a quarter of their sleep time in REM sleep, about the same amount as an adult.

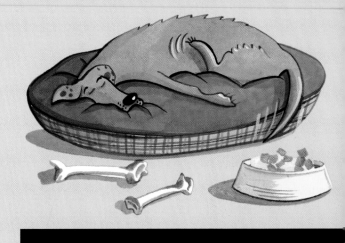

You can recognize the rapid eye movements of REM sleep in someone else — or in a pet. Watch a cat or dog while it is sleeping (but don't disturb it). Check the pet after it's been asleep for 10 to 20 minutes. Can you see its eyeballs darting back and forth under its eyelids?

How long did the REM period last? The pet may growl or twitch its ears or paws as it dreams. Did your sleeper move any other part of its body during that time?

Sweet Dreams

You're at the Olympic Games. The crowd cheers as you kneel at the starting line of the 100-meter dash. You check out the competition and see Bluebeard the Pirate crouched in one lane and your pet goldfish in another. As the starting gun fires, you realize something — a dozen television crews are filming you.

Sound strange? Not if you know it's a dream — one of those strange stories your brain makes up while you're in REM sleep. Everyone dreams. Most people dream for about an hour every night during REM sleep. We dream in other stages of sleep, too, but those dreams are about fairly normal things, and people seem to forget those more easily. Some people don't remember any of their dreams at all. And although people dream in color, some only remember the dream adventures in black and white. Color seems to be the first thing to fade from memory.

- We dream what we see. Researchers asked volunteers to wear goggles with red-tinted lenses 24 hours a day. Each morning, the volunteers described their dreams. Within a few days all the dream objects they reported were red.

The Dreamer's Body

While you're in non-REM sleep, you are relaxed and calm. But your body seems to switch to high alert when you enter REM sleep. Your heart and breathing may suddenly speed up. Your eyes dart around as though you're "watching" your dream take place. Your brainwaves look a lot like they do when you're awake. In fact, your whole body behaves much like it does when you're awake, with one very big difference — you can't move. At all. Your closed eyes dart around and you may twitch a little, but you never move. You are paralyzed. Unless something very scary or startling happens in a dream that shocks you awake, you lie perfectly still until your dream is over. This is called REM sleep paralysis, or atonia.

While you're sleeping, your brain sends messages to your arms and legs to move, just like when you're awake. But in REM sleep, something keeps those messages from reaching their destination. Atonia prevents you from acting out what's happening in your dream. It may also be why some dreamers feel rooted to the spot.

Try these tips to help you remember your dreams. Be sure to have a pen and paper beside your bed.

1. Before you go to sleep, tell yourself you're going to have a dream and you're going to remember it.

2. When you wake up, lie quietly for a few minutes and see what thoughts enter your head. Write down any dream snippets you remember.

3. A few times during the day, read over the snippets. Write down any new dream details that you remember.

Why We Dream

If you were sick thousands of years ago in ancient Greece, you might have visited a dream oracle for advice on how to get better. The oracle would perform a ceremony and then put you to bed on a specially prepared sheepskin. When you awoke, you'd describe your dream, and the oracle would figure out what the symbols in your dream meant and declare the cure for your illness.

Through the ages, people have had many different ideas about why we dream. The people of ancient India believed that dreams let them glimpse the world they would go to after they died. And the Senoi people in the jungles of Malaysia used to believe that their dreams warned them of problems or conflicts so that they could avoid them.

Scientists still don't know for sure why we dream, but they have some ideas. One theory is that dreams may be a form of exercise that helps the brain develop.

• Birds may dream, too! Bird brainwaves indicate that they go into REM sleep, but only for five or six seconds. Still, that may be long enough to dream. When researchers played a recording of birds singing for some "dreaming" birds, the area of their brain that controls singing generated a lot of electrical signals — as if the birds were dreaming about singing back.

Dreaming and Memory

You've been working at your computer for two hours. Your project is half done. Just to be safe, you hit the "save" command before continuing. The computer begins transferring information from the file you've been working on into its permanent memory. Dreaming could be your brain's way of doing exactly what your computer just did.

Some scientists believe that your short-term memory — the part that lets you remember things for a day or so — holds all the new information during the day. Then at night, as you dream, your brain sifts through the day's experiences. It stores the important details in your long-term memory and tosses out the rest, perhaps straight into your dreams.

Scientists haven't yet found a way to prove this theory, but one thing is certain — dreaming IS important. If you are prevented from dreaming, your brain makes up for it by getting extra dream sleep the first chance it can.

You Try It

Next time you remember part of a dream, try to figure out if any of the details came from something that happened that day. Maybe the gorilla on a skateboard came from zoo pictures you saw in the newspaper and the new skateboard you've been wanting. Or maybe you dreamed you were bald because you noticed that a friend got a haircut.

What Dreams Mean

One night in 1865, the German chemist Friedrich Kekulé was trying to figure out the shape and structure of the chemical benzene. Frustrated, he settled into his chair for a nap and dreamed of a snake with its tail in its mouth. When he woke up, he realized his dream held the answer — the molecules of benzene form a ring.

Many creative people say they find inspiration in dreams. The eighteenth-century composer Wolfgang Amadeus Mozart claimed that the music he composed was music he heard in his dreams. After he woke up, he simply wrote down the notes.

Do all dreams, like those of Mozart and Kekulé, hold some important information for the dreamer? Or are dreams really just random thoughts? Some scientists suggest that the electric energy buzzing around inside your head as you sleep happens to stimulate certain areas of your brain, bringing random details to mind. Your dreams may be the stories your brain creates by joining these details together. Is this true? No one knows for sure.

- The echidna, an Australian hedgehog, is one of the only mammals that has no REM sleep, and so probably doesn't dream. It has a very large brain for an animal its size, and scientists wonder if the extra space holds all the junk it can't throw out in dreams.

It's All in Your Head

In 1900, a German doctor named Sigmund Freud published his famous book, **The Interpretation of Dreams**. He was the first person to suggest that the details and events in a dream might have a deeper meaning. For instance, if you dream of yelling at a small, white dog, it could be because you're angry with someone who is short and blond. Freud believed that by analyzing dreams, he could help people recognize feelings they didn't know they had.

What an object or event in a dream means, Freud and others said, depends a lot on the person dreaming it. Still, there are some standard dream symbols that many people apply to their dreams. If you dream of:
• flying, you feel confident
• falling, it could mean you are worried about failing, perhaps at school
• being naked, you may be feeling helpless or self-conscious about something
• a king and queen, they may represent your parents
• a road or path, it may be a symbol of your journey through life

Things that Go Bump in the Night

Long ago, many people thought bad dreams were caused by visits from an evil spirit. That's where the word "nightmare" comes from — in Old English, "mare" means demon.

People of all ages have nightmares, but we dream our scariest ones when we are three or four years old. Experts think this is because that's when our imaginations are forming, and we may have trouble telling what's real from what's not real. For some reason, girls have more nightmares than boys.

Most nightmares occur during the second half of the night, when we are getting more REM sleep. In a nightmare, you feel threatened and in danger. REM sleep paralysis (see page 21) can make a scary nightmare even scarier, because you feel you can't move a muscle to protect yourself. If the fright is strong enough, it may break through the paralysis, allowing you to move. That's why you usually remember the most frightening nightmares — your fear was great enough to wake you up. Most experts think people have nightmares when they are afraid of, or worried about, something.

- Kids sometimes have a kind of bad dream called a night terror. They sit up and scream in fear, but even though their eyes are wide open, they're really still asleep. After several minutes, the fear passes and the sleeper usually just lies back down to sleep — and remembers nothing about it in the morning.

Acting out Dreams

A man dreams he's a football player who's running, jumping and dodging other players. When he wakes up, he finds his bedroom furniture is broken in pieces all around him. Like a small number of others, mostly men over 50, this man has what's called REM sleep disorder. For him, REM sleep paralysis doesn't kick in. The brain's messages for movement, which normally don't reach people's arms and legs during dreams, actually **do** get there. That means the person can walk, run, dive, or do just about anything. So when the sleeper dreams he is running to jump onto a moving train, he will run and fling himself onto whatever is near him.

People with REM sleep disorder don't act out every dream — perhaps only one every few months. Some dreams involve harmless activities, but the dreams can be violent. People with REM sleep disorder often end up with broken bones, cuts and bruises.

You Try It

How can you get rid of a nightmare that keeps coming back? Give this a try.

1. Write down everything you can remember about the nightmare.

2. Think up a happy ending.

3. In your mind, go over your dream with its new happy ending. Describe it to someone else or try writing it down. Think about it before you go to bed.

Tossing and Turning

Almost everyone has insomnia (in-SOM-nee-yuh) — trouble sleeping — once in a while. If you're worried about a test, upset with a friend or excited about a trip, your mind may be too busy thinking about it to sleep. Once the problem or event passes, so does the insomnia. Some people, however, have insomnia almost every night, and they may need a doctor's help to solve their sleep problems.

Insomnia isn't the only problem that can keep you tossing and turning. Imagine lying in bed ready to sleep. Just as you relax, you feel a creepy, prickly feeling in the calves of your legs — like ants marching up and down your skin. The feeling gets worse and worse until you can't stand it. You have to get up and walk around.

Ah, relief! But when you lie back down, the creeping returns. Finally, after hours of frustration, you fall asleep. That's what bedtime can be like for the ten percent of people who have Restless Legs Syndrome.

Many people with Restless Legs also have a disorder called Periodic Limb Movements in Sleep (PLMS). While they're asleep, their legs suddenly start jerking a couple of times every minute. Each jerk comes exactly the same number of seconds after the last. Although they don't remember the jerks, each one wakes them up slightly, and in the morning they feel exhausted. PLMS is most common in people over 65, but some younger adults and children have it as well.

Snoring the Night Away

It's night, thousands of years ago. Some early humans are asleep in a cave. A predator smells them and prepares to attack. Suddenly, a loud snore echoes through the cave. The predator hesitates, then decides to look for less dangerous prey. Snoring may have protected our ancient ancestors from fearsome creatures, but today, for most people, it's just a bothersome nighttime noise.

Over 25 percent of men and 15 percent of women snore every night. When a snorer takes a breath, his tongue, his uvula (that thing you see hanging in your throat) and parts of his throat vibrate. All these vibrations make that familiar raspy sound.

Very loud snoring may be a sign of a serious problem called obstructive sleep apnea. An apnea sufferer may stop breathing for up to 60 seconds before he gasps and snorts himself awake enough to take a breath. Some people do this hundreds of times a night, but they don't remember and have no idea why they are so sleepy during the day. Being tired isn't the only problem. The lack of oxygen during the night makes the sleeper's heart work harder and can cause high blood pressure and even a heart attack or stroke.

Not all snorers are in danger. As long as the snoring is steady with no long pauses or snorts, the snorer probably doesn't have obstructive sleep apnea.

- The loudest snore ever recorded reached 93 decibels. That's as loud as an electric blender, a ringing alarm clock or a dog barking just an arm's length away from you.

Sleepwalkers •••

It was the middle of the night when an 11-year-old boy got up out of his bed. He headed for the front door and opened it. And then he was gone. The next morning, his parents were astonished to find his bed empty — and even more surprised when he turned up unharmed 160 km (100 mi.) from home! Was he kidnapped? Did he run away? No, he was sleepwalking. He walked from the house to the nearby railway tracks and climbed aboard a train that carried him out of town.

About 3 kids out of every 20 sleepwalk at least once. Most outgrow it by the time they're 14. Sleepwalking usually happens in the first two hours of the night, during deep sleep (Stage 3 or 4). Some sleepers just sit up in bed. Others walk around. Their eyes are open, but they're not aware of people around them. They often go back to bed after wandering around for up to 30 minutes, and they don't remember a thing about it in the morning. Most sleepwalkers are so deeply asleep, it's best not to try to wake them.

••• **Sleeptalkers**

What do sleeptalkers talk about? Probably not their dreams, since sleeptalking almost never occurs during REM sleep. Often a person listening to a sleeptalker can't make out any real words. It's usually just muttering and mumbo-jumbo. Many adults talk in their sleep, and even more children do. If you talk to a child shortly after she falls asleep, she will probably say something. If two children share a bedroom, the sound of one of them sleeptalking will sometimes get the other talking, too. Of course, you couldn't call it a conversation since neither has a clue what the other is saying!

Don't step on the frog

Your nose looks like a banana

• Gorillas who have learned sign language have been known to make signs for words while they are asleep.

Walks on the Wild Side

Most sleepwalkers end up back in bed. But some don't. Sleepwalkers have been found the next morning snoozing in the bathtub or under the kitchen table. One man went to bed in his room at a hotel and woke to find himself downstairs in the lobby in his pajamas.

Sleepwalking can also involve more than just walking. Sleepwalkers sometimes look through drawers, get dressed or even take down curtains. It's very common for sleepwalking children to walk to a garbage pail, toy box or other object that reminds them of a toilet and — ahem — use it!

Sleep Attack!

A fisherman out on his boat settled into a routine. He cast the line, waited, reeled it in, cast the line again. Then he got a nibble. But before he could reel in his catch, he fell asleep. With a mighty tug, the fish pulled him right out of the boat into the water!

It sounds strange for a person to fall asleep in the middle of doing something, but it happens all the time to people who have narcolepsy (NAR-ko-lep-see). This sleep disorder makes people fall asleep two, three or even twenty times each day, even if they've slept eight or more hours the night before. A sleep attack can overtake them when they're doing almost anything and can last anywhere from 30 seconds to 30 minutes.

People with narcolepsy usually start having sleep attacks as teenagers, but some children have attacks as well. No one really knows why narcolepsy happens. Part of the answer may be that the sleep of these people isn't the same as that of regular sleepers. Narcolepsy sufferers don't drift down through Stages 1 to 4 of non-REM sleep, like most people do. Instead, they go directly into REM sleep and move on to the other stages later in their sleep cycle.

Attacked by Atonia

Many people with narcolepsy also have to cope with cataplexy (CA-tuh-pleks-ee). Remember atonia, the paralysis that takes over your body during REM sleep? In most people with narcolepsy, that paralysis can suddenly be triggered even when they're awake. This creates cataplectic attacks. Whenever the person has strong emotions — for some, happiness or excitement; for others, anger or surprise — their muscles go limp. They may even collapse on the ground and lie there for a few minutes, awake but with their arms and legs completely paralyzed.

- **Ever heard of sleeping sickness? It's a tropical disease that makes you feel tired all the time. It's caused by a parasite that gets into your bloodstream, usually from the bite of a tsetse fly.**
  - **Some animals have narcolepsy, too. Stanford University researchers even bred a whole kennel of narcoleptic dobermans so that they could study them.**

Sitting Bull

In 1977, the bull-fighting industry in Spain had a big problem. Bulls would charge in to the arena — and fall down. Then they'd get up — and fall down again. The fans were outraged.

Eventually, the organizers stopped using the falling-down bulls to breed new ones, and the problem disappeared. Quite likely, the bulls had narcolepsy and were having cataplectic attacks due to the excitement of the fight.

A Good Night's Sleep

When's the last time you complained about your bedtime? Last night? It just never seems fair that kids have to go to sleep while adults stay up later. Unfortunately for kids, the grown-ups have scientific research backing them up. Generally, the younger you are the more sleep you need to keep your growing body and your developing brain working well. If you don't get enough sleep, you'll feel cranky and unhappy, be more likely to get sick and have a much harder time learning new things.

As people get older, their need for sleep drops. But there's one big exception. For reasons doctors and scientists don't completely understand yet, many teenagers seem to need more sleep than they did at age 11 — perhaps because of the major changes their bodies go through at puberty.

How much sleep is enough?

Age	Hours of sleep needed a day
1 week	16 to 18 hours
1 year	12 to 14 hours
5 years	10 to 12 hours
7 years	9 to 11 hours
11 years	8 to 10 hours
teenager	9 to 10 hours
adult	7 to 9 hours

Lots of people don't get enough sleep. Doctors, firefighters, police officers and many others often go a full day and night with no sleep at all. You'd think they'd feel drowsy but an emergency or an interesting activity can keep even very overtired people awake and alert.

In 1965, a San Diego high school student named Randy Gardner stayed awake for 264 hours — 11 days — to set a new record. Even when he was at his sleepiest, playing some basketball was enough to wake him right up.

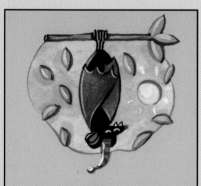

- Not all animals need the same amount of sleep. Giraffes and elephants get along with only 3 hours, while pet cats sleep 16 hours and bats sleep 20 hours.

You Try It

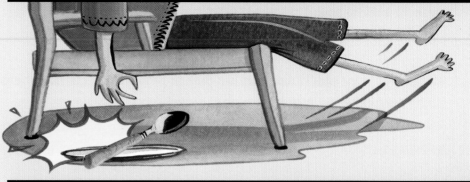

Are you getting enough sleep? Try this experiment between 2 P.M. and 4 P.M. to help you find out. Challenge others in your family to try it, too.

1. Sit comfortably in an armchair with one arm over the side. Make sure there are no loud noises, people or other distractions near you.

2. Place a plate on the floor below your hand.

3. Hold a spoon loosely in that hand.

4. Check the time, then relax and try to sleep.

5. If you fall asleep, your hand will relax and the spoon will clatter onto the plate, waking you up. Check the time.

The quicker you fell asleep, the more nighttime sleep you should be getting. If you're still awake with spoon in hand after 20 minutes, you're probably getting the right amount of sleep each night.

Sleeping in Strange Places

Where's the strangest place a person could sleep? Space is definitely high on the list. Astronauts orbiting Earth tuck themselves into a sort of sleeping bag hanging from the shuttle wall, or a tiny cubicle the size of a coffin. Since there's no gravity, they don't quite feel like they're lying down. For one thing, their arms keep floating up in front of their faces! No wonder most astronauts lose between one and three hours of sleep each night that they're in space.

In Your Own Bed

Most people sleep best in familiar surroundings. Lying down in your own bed seems to let you relax more completely and get enough deep sleep, the kind that helps you feel rested and refreshed.

Changing beds or even sleeping positions can make a big difference. For example, ever try to sleep sitting up? Chances are you got very little deep sleep. Your brain knows when you're upright. In fact, it may be trying to protect you by keeping you from relaxing completely so that you won't fall down and hurt yourself.

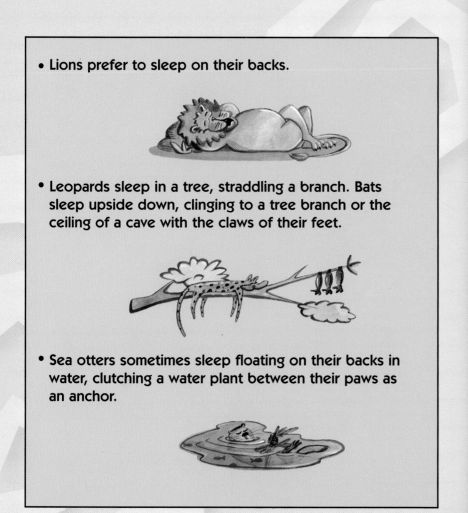

- **Lions prefer to sleep on their backs.**

- **Leopards sleep in a tree, straddling a branch. Bats sleep upside down, clinging to a tree branch or the ceiling of a cave with the claws of their feet.**

- **Sea otters sometimes sleep floating on their backs in water, clutching a water plant between their paws as an anchor.**

Do you sleep better when everything is familiar? Ask a parent to check on you two nights in a row (about every five minutes or so) to see how long it takes you to fall asleep. The first night, sleep the way you usually do. The next night, follow the same bedtime routine, but change WHERE you sleep — maybe switch beds or sleep with your head at the foot end. Did you fall asleep as quickly the second night?

Famous Sleepers

The inventor Thomas Edison thought sleep was a huge waste of time. He believed that if he conquered darkness, he could free up many hours for work. In a way, he was right. In 1910, before Edison invented the lightbulb, young adults slept about nine hours each night. Now, thanks to Edison's lightbulb, people stay up longer and sleep only seven hours a night. That means adults are awake for about 700 more hours each year.

Edison himself claimed he slept only four hours a night. But he often took two naps of three hours each during the day. Experts say the naps boosted his creativity and probably helped him invent the very thing that keeps the rest of us awake. In fact, they say napping for as little as 20 minutes can improve a person's abilities for the next 10 hours.

- Animals nap, too. Some birds take mini naps of 30 seconds or so while flying. That's how they manage to fly non-stop during long migrations.

- Porpoises and bottle-nosed dolphins breathe air, yet sleep underwater. At night, half their brain stays alert enough to get them to the surface to breathe. Every two hours or so through the night, the sleeping side of the brain awakes and the other side gets its chance to sleep.

Notable Nappers

The French Emperor Napoleon Bonaparte always went to bed at 10 P.M., but was usually up again by 2 A.M. He'd work at his desk until 5 A.M. and then nap until 7 A.M. Winston Churchill, the former British prime minister, did almost the opposite. He usually worked late, until 3 or 4 A.M., and then slept until 8 A.M. Then he took a two-hour nap in the afternoon.

Leonardo da Vinci, the famous artist and scientist, may have been the most interesting napper. According to folklore, he never got a full night's sleep. He just napped for 15 minutes every four hours — a total of just one and a half hours of sleep a day! Experiments have shown that da Vinci's 90 minutes of sleep aren't enough to survive on for more than three or four days. Still, da Vinci may have used this napping strategy when he was racing to finish a project, such as when he was dissecting human bodies to study anatomy. He would've had just three or four days to dissect a body before it became badly decomposed.

Not all famous thinkers are nappers. The brilliant scientist Albert Einstein loved to sleep. He said he was at his best only when he got 10 hours of sleep a night.

Larks and Owls

Most adults go to sleep between 10 P.M. and midnight and wake up between 6 and 7:30 A.M. But some people, nicknamed "larks," feel tired shortly after supper. They go to bed early and rise the next morning with the sun, full of energy. Other people are called "owls" because they stay up late and don't feel fully awake until mid-morning.

Index

Better Homes and Gardens®

Creative
Table Settings

The colonial bouquet above is color-keyed to harmonize with the hostess' china and crystal. The same containers are used both for candle holders and flowers. Because the table settings reflect the tranquil spirit that prevails, the total effect is one of graciousness and elegance.

BETTER HOMES AND GARDENS BOOKS

Editorial Director: Don Dooley
Managing Editor: Malcolm E. Robinson   Art Director: John Berg
Assistant Managing Editor: Lawrence D. Clayton
Assistant Art Director: Randall Yontz
Senior Editor: Marie Schulz
Designers: Harijs Priekulis, Tonya Rodriguez
Contributing Editor: Jane Cornell
Consultant: Fae Huttenlocher

CONTENTS

Introduction

"Invest mealtime with charm and grace, add to it an attractive setting, and the simplest meal becomes a delightful adventure....Such meals lend a special something to the happiness of family life, a vital influence on manners of the growing generation, and a social occasion to which the guests look forward with pleasant anticipation."

"Gracious dining must be a part of everyday living, not just kept for company affairs. Its secret is neither costly detail nor elaborate procedure, but a harmony of settings and appointments and a knowledge of simple, correct service. And always the 'right' and 'wrong' in table settings is founded not on the dictates of some superficial custom, but on the comfort, pleasure, and courtesy due those seated at the table."

The above, which was written 30 years ago by Better Homes and Gardens table settings editor, Fae Huttenlocher — she also provided invaluable assistance on this up-to-the-minute book — is just as timely today as it was in 1944.

The only conspicuous change is that today most people have adopted a more casual life-style — both with table settings and entertaining habits. You can more readily break those hard-and-fast rules, especially with the new techniques and new materials that make tableware more beautiful, more durable, and easy to maintain.

But this does not mean that you can't use the white or ivory damask table linens, fine china dinnerware, crystal stemware with its clear distinctive 'ring', and gleaming flatware. These are still for formal parties, but you can use this tableware with today's informal parties—brunches, buffets, and cocktail parties. And now you can use them more adventurously.

Be flexible—mix and match colors, patterns, textures, and materials. Create the mood that pleases you most. If your tastes lean toward traditional, country, or contemporary furnishings, reflect the same spirit in your table settings.

Table linens have experienced 'growing pains,' too. Hard-to-iron tablecloths and napkins have given way to ones made of carefree permanent-press fabrics. Colorful place mats and table runners have gained wide acceptance from busy homemakers. You can even make your own table linens and take pride in presenting a tabletop setting that is truly original.

Centerpieces and table decorations have become more important, too. There's something about a table that has some sort of decoration that makes dining more pleasant. It doesn't have to be large or lavish.

Above all, don't let your meals become just daily chores that must be tended to. Instead, treat your menu planning, food preparation, and table setting tasks with wholehearted enthusiasm.

Table Settings

The three elements that determine the ultimate success of your table settings are your planned fare, the furnishings that you have in your home, and personal flair. As such, creative table setting styles are reflections of your life-style.

Try matching your settings to your meals. For example, use earthenware dishes rather than highly decorated fine china when serving lusty peasant-type food. Or, make a 'special occasion' cake more impressive by employing your best china and silver. You can make any meal more exciting with proper presentation.

Most table appointments reflect design periods, as does furniture. Coordinate your table settings to your furnishings. However, a table setting that is a departure from the general tone of your home, especially for a party, might give the necessary zest to the occasion. Remember that the change-of-pace should be striking, not shocking.

← *Daily dining can be grand, especially if your table setting is in keeping with the furniture. Split centerpieces in welcoming orange tones create intimacy and can be used for many meals.*

Test your table setting flair on your family first. Since mealtime is the one time when most families are all together, why not dress the table for the occasion?

Start with the meal that is most important in your house. Sunday supper stars in many homes. In others, breakfast is the meal most often shared by all of the family members. In still others, the after-church meal gathers the family together. Your table setting, if planned carefully and skillfully, can make this family meal a real occasion.

Be realistic in assessing your entertaining patterns. If frequent sit-down dinners are your forte, you should have a superb set of dinnerware with all the individual place pieces and corresponding flatware and glassware. If buffet gatherings are more your speed, you'll be much better off with plenty of large platter plates and all-purpose glasses.

After you have tested some exciting table settings on your family, use the successful ones for company. A ready repertoire of table settings banishes any last-minute panics when unexpected guests do arrive. Being prepared will give any hostess confidence. It will also ensure that you can spend time with your guests.

Styles of Table Settings

Table settings allow you to take a design journey into the past and to many foreign lands. In a home decorated according to a specific period or country, researching the exact styles of table appointments that are appropriate can be both fun and a spark to creativity. The end of your search is the table setting that delights you, your family, and your guests.

Many contemporary table appointments are up-dated versions of designs that were first introduced during the flourishing of a great cultural age. Renaissance, Louis XIV, Louis XV, Early American, and even modern are examples of eras that are represented in current tabletop designs. The test of time has shown that the old elements originally used with period furniture are indeed striking.

But don't limit yourself to these tried-and-true designs. They should serve only as a springboard for creativity, because it is the personal elements that truly bring a table setting to life.

For example, a trip to Europe or 'south of the border' can serve as the inspiration of a table setting. The incredible increase of travel in the last quarter century has allowed many people to see the styles of decorating of other lands firsthand. But, the import of furnishings and accessories from other lands means that you can indulge in your dreamland fantasies without ever setting foot outside our national boundaries. Your table can represent the melting pot history of the country.

The three main categories of table setting styles are traditional; contemporary, which

Louis XV tableware reflects the sumptuousness of the French court with curves, scrolls, and flowers decorating vermeil flatware. The otherwise unadorned stemware and dinnerware are accented only with an etched gold border.

Chippendale introduced the simplicity of Chinese design to furnishings in the eighteenth century. Patterned plates and sleekly curved flatware and glassware fit his mood. You can use Chippendale tableware in almost any decor.

can be either formal or casual; and country casual. Decide first which of these looks you like the most.

Traditional Table Settings

Often called classics, these designs have a certain formality and ornamental detail inspired by a number of ancient sources, notably early Greece and Rome.

Typical of the plate styles are scrolled rims or borders and patterns including wreaths, scrolls, and floral designs. Glassware, almost invariably stemware, is characterized by a pure and stately silhouette. Usually, the glassware is elaborately ornamented with designs that are either cut or etched, and with edgings of gold or silver. Flatware runs the gamut from simple patterns, such as the fiddleback classic from the eighteenth century, to richly decorated styles, popular during the Baroque period. These often had scrolls and garlands of flowers engraved on them.

Maintain the look of luxury of this style by using highly decorated cloths in such quality fabrics as damask, embroidered linen, or lace in white or off-white.

Beloved renditions of formal styles include settings in Louis XV, Chippendale, and Queen Anne. All of these use appointments that can be found in a local store; nevertheless, they are rich in the design heritage of the elegant past.

Colorful Contemporary

This style is expressed in simplicity without sterility at the table. Contemporary tableware may be decorated or unadorned, formal or informal. Its bold colors, dramatic accents, and clean lines combine to give it a dramatic impact.

Some contemporary dinnerware patterns are sleek and smooth, others have a textural interest that is created with the glaze—often crackled or crazed. Sometimes, a design is carved on the surface.

Queen Anne design, with its gentle curves, lends itself to many tabletop possibilities. The patterned vermeil flatware, etched crystal, gold-banded china, and floral damask cloth are adaptable to almost any dining room decor.

Contemporary tableware is pure in form. This black and white dinnerware is starkly unadorned. Team it with a dotted table cover, textured napkins, chunky goblets and, for a change of pace, ornately patterned flatware.

Contemporary flatware is an abrupt departure from the traditional shapes of the past. Asymmetrical handle designs are often used, as are sleekly simple, undecorated pieces. The current trend is toward adding some decoration to relieve the starkness of otherwise plain patterns.

Often, modern glassware is brilliantly colored or uniquely shaped. Unusual stems, variations in the thickness of the glass, and departures from the traditional shapes make modern glassware exciting. Abstract designs or symmetrical patterns can be worked directly into the glass or can be applied as decoration. They are either formal or informal, but always stylized and striking.

There are virtually no limits in the variety of design in contemporary linens. In the case of glass tables, having no linens at all is perfectly acceptable. For some contemporary tableware, use solid colors with great textural interest. Brilliant patterns, usually with strong geometric themes, are good modern matchmates. Since modern patterned cloths are often so strong, complement them with solid napkins, or vice-versa, and cover contemporary tables with modern materials such as mirrors or plexiglass.

Take inspiration for modern settings from any period, when form follows function. Scandinavian design, the Bauhaus school of the 1930s, and Shaker furnishings all have this orientation. In a Norwegian setting, relieve a stark black and white scheme with terra cotta and the decoration of the flatware. And accent the clean lines of white ware and pewter for Shaker with a table cover with simple stripes.

Country Casual Table Settings

These are the most popular of all settings. They lend themselves to daily dining, and have a warmth that echoes the hearthside of the past. With the exception of highly styled formal furnishings, almost any kind of interior can readily support a country style of table setting.

Shaker design has utilitarian simplicity that makes it equally at home in country or contemporary table settings. The pewter, stainless, white glass ceramic dinnerware, and no-press striped cloth have beauty and clean cut lines.

Early American is this country's most popular country setting. Hearthside tones and simple flatware, bulky crafted candles, and a home-loomed-look cloth are combined. Terra-cotta pottery always bespeaks casual.

Country appointments and accessories are generally less expensive than those for other table styles. A collection of less-expensive pieces can yield endless variations on the country theme. This is also an ideal spot for using any crafts, homemade or otherwise. A beautiful country setting can have just as much panache as the most elaborate and ornate formal traditional setting. In fact, some style leaders prefer a beautiful casual setting for their entertaining because it is both warm and inviting.

Country covers a range of styles, from Early American through South American and casual Mediterranean or Spanish. The key element in defining this style is informal dinnerware. Heavy pottery, earthenware, ironstone, and stoneware fall into this category. Decorations are floral or geometric.

Casual flatware can echo the rustic simplicity of Early American tinware or be decorated with modern motifs. Light traditional flowers and garlands also mix well with casual floral-patterned plates.

Heavy, short-stemmed goblets suit this style. Milk glass is an American classic. There are many contemporary patterns in pressed and molded crystal that can be used to dress updated combinations.

Pewter, copper, or brass hollow ware often is used on a casual table instead of more formal silverplate. Rough-weaved textures and hand-printed looks coordinate best with the heavier dining pieces. Formal linens or fragile glassware would be heavily outweighed by casual dinnerware.

Contemporary casseroles in colorful enamel fit the casual table perfectly and are ideal for the one-dish meal.

Eclectic Mixing and Matching

This trend reflects that there are no hard-and-fast rules to restrict a table to one style. While current table appointments reflect specific design periods, most are modified to fit into many moods. This allows the juxtaposing of designs.

A Mexican setting, although casually inspired, takes on elegant tones through a no-color scheme. Grillwork inspired the flatware handles; Aztec geometrics, the craft-look cloth. This suits both modern and Mediterranean.

A Peruvian-inspired setting combines butterscotch, black, and ruby. Use the natural colors of South America and our west as a wonderful source for casual table settings. Grand Canyon colors translate to almost any table.

Formal Table Settings

The soft glow of candlelight gleaming on best crystal, silver, and elegant dinnerware connotes a formal table setting. The care with which the hostess plans and executes this special setting makes any formal setting out of the ordinary.

Your best table service need not be reserved for only rare holiday occasions. Liberate yours as often as you like, for with reasonable care it will last more than a lifetime with fairly frequent use.

To a purist, no dinner is formal unless served to seated guests. Place plates are used and set at each place for effect and then removed. And the bread-and-butter plate is eliminated entirely.

Today, more relaxed settings are considered formal, including sit-down dinners and self-served buffets. The latter is less formal. Both call for a full tablecloth, flowers, and candles.

Sit-Down Dinners

The size of the table dictates the number of guests you can accommodate at a sit-down formal dinner. Allow 20 to 30 inches for each place setting, depending upon the amount of flatware to be used, and whether or not side plates are planned. Usually, no more than eight can be seated comfortably. This also seems to be the magic number for congenial conversation.

Place the plate and flatware about one inch from the table's edge, forks to the left, knives and spoons to the right. However, lay the shrimp-cocktail fork to the right of the plate. Arrange these pieces in the order of use, from the outside in. This makes it easy for guests to choose the proper implement. Dessert service is not placed on the table. Place the carving set at the host's right hand.

How to set the table for a formal sit-down dinner

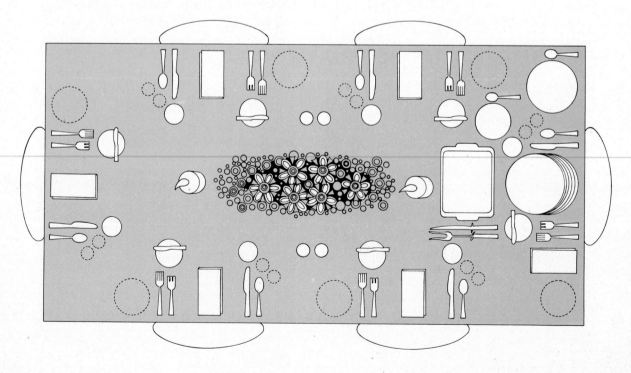

The traditional dining room above is a perfect setting for a formal dinner. The richly radiant color scheme stems from the patterned, Oriental dinnerware and is enhanced by the centerpiece of red roses. Etched crystal and elaborate flatware round out the formal mood.

A napkin, folded vertically, lies at the left of the forks. If the setting includes a salad plate, put the napkin in the center of the dinner or service plate.

The water goblet belongs just above the tip of the knife. Set the wine goblet diagonally to the right. Place a second wine above and between the two so that the three goblets form a triangle.

Put the salad plate to the left of the forks, with the bread-and-butter plate above them. The butter spreader lies parallel to the edge, or is positioned diagonally, handle to the plate and blade facing the edge. Individual salts and peppers go either above each plate or between two diners. Set cigarette and match holders above the plate. Center a place card on each guest's napkin or in a decorative special holder.

Make sure that candle flames are above the eye level of your guests or right on the table. They add glamour to the setting, but should only be lit after dusk. Usually, they flank a centerpiece. Although white candles are usually considered to be more formal than colored candles, either kind is acceptable on the modern formal table of today. Candles always add greatly to the general scheme of a dinner.

The dimensions of a centerpiece for a formal sit-down table are a most important factor. To ensure that the centerpiece will in no way impede conversation, be sure to keep it low. Usually, it is centered on the table. Often, the centerpiece is coordinated with the color of the cloth. More muted shades will complement fine table appointments better than bold colors will.

14

Buffet Dinners

Although they are by nature informal, buffet dinners can be just as elegant in tone as a formal dinner if you take care to use the right table appointments and table decorations. Candles, a full-length tablecloth, and a centerpiece will accent the beauty of your best china, crystal, and silver. An elegant buffet dinner is the perfect solution for serving more people than could be comfortably seated around your dining table, and your guests will enjoy it.

Most of the decorations and food can be prepared far in advance for a well-conceived buffet. Use the best of both worlds by setting a buffet dinner, complemented with tables for seating. Arrange borrowed card tables throughout the house, and decorate them in keeping with the main table. This dining plan allows for the serving of almost any type of food. If dinner plates are to be balanced by the guests, be sure to plan a menu consisting of foods that need no cutting, and with no hazardous liquid sauces.

The convenience of the guest is the main consideration in planning a buffet. It determines the kind of service to be used by each person. Plates should be large enough to hold a main course, relishes, vegetable, salad, and rolls. Only one glass can be handled—either a water glass or a wine goblet. Flatware should be limited to a dinner fork and either a butter spreader or a dinner knife because they must remain on the plate. Napkins should be as large as possible, since the plates will be held on the lap—unless you use folding trays or small tables. The latter two are much more comfortable than balancing a plate.

For large groups, center the table with twin arrangements of plates, food, silver, and napkins on each side. Suggest that guests form two lines to help themselves. If space does not permit, place the table near a wall, leaving enough room behind it so that the hostess can walk comfortably there to replenish the servings of food. Beverages placed on a tea cart or a buffet server will eliminate unnecessary clutter on the main table.

How to set the table for a buffet meal

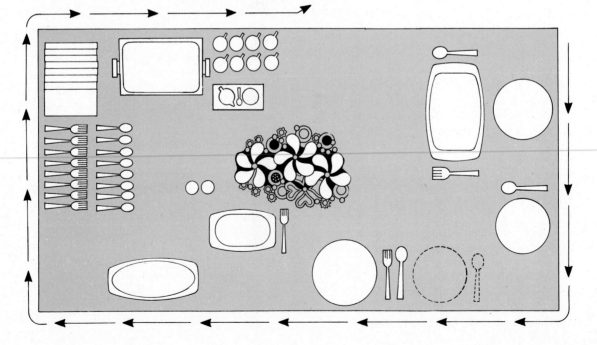

This formal buffet table has a vine-covered trellis behind and a centerpiece of fruits and flowers. This lavish background makes the food even more delectable and enhances the beauty of the elegant serving pieces, the floor-length table cover, china, flatware, and crystal.

The logical sequence of serving oneself determines the layout of the table. Pick the point at which guests should begin. Plates come first, then the main course, (usually at the end of the table). Then, other foods such as vegetables, rolls, and relishes go along the table. Make sure that dishes requiring two hands for serving, such as a tossed salad, have space adjacent to them for the guests to set down their plates while they are serving themselves. Flatware and napkins come at the last so that the guests need not carry them the length of the table.

During the dinner, make sure that food is replenished and kept either warm or cold. Also, circulate among the guests, offering rolls or refilling wine or water glasses. Placing coasters near each guest's setting is both thoughtful and practical.

Formal buffet decorations can be as large or as high as you wish, especially if the table is placed against the wall. You don't have to worry about a tall floral centerpiece hindering conversation, as you would at a sit-down dinner. Take advantage of this freedom to be exuberantly creative. However, make sure that the decorations do not detract from the food. Incorporate existing wall decorations, or consider adding ones especially for the party. Sheeting or additional tablecloths dropped to the floor below the main cloth's 15-inch drop are quite dramatic. The arrangement stays through the table's second setup for dessert and beverages.

Make any seating tables mini-formal echoes for a sit-down buffet. Arrange flatware, linens, and candles according to the same rules as for a formal sit-down dinner.

Teas and Receptions

One of the most delightful traditions in table setting is the afternoon tea or reception. This social convention serves a number of hostessing situations. A tea can be as elegant as a formal dinner, but far less expensive. It is also an ideal way to gather together acquaintances.

Teas are called receptions when this party format is used to introduce or honor one or more persons. New neighbors, new business associates, and new brides are often honored with a reception.

Small teas are usually for women only, while larger ones can be mixed. The hours are socially prescribed; teas are scheduled in the afternoon between the hours of four and six. Invitations should cover at least one and a half hours. The arrival of guests is usually staggered, making this party ideal for a large guest list.

For a large tea, set a large table with your prettiest cloth, or cover two small tables with floor-length cloths. Shining silver and china, family best, can be beautifully displayed on a tea table. Your tea service should be immaculate. Since the affair spans dusk, light the candles. As always, an inventive centerpiece can set the theme of the table. If the tea is in honor of a special occasion, use this as the theme.

It is customary to serve two beverages at a large tea. In addition to the tea drink, serve a light punch or coffee. The tea service and its accompaniments, sugar and creamer, small salver of lemons daintily sliced or wedged, small serving fork, sugar tongs, and optionally, a tea strainer and waste bowl, sit at one end of the table. The other beverage is at the other end. Set cups and saucers on the left, teaspoons and napkins on the right, with food platters set in easy reach along the length of the table.

Friends are usually flattered when asked to pour, as long as they are relieved after an hour. You can serve a small tea by yourself. Guests help themselves to light foods such as petite sandwiches, cookies, petit fours, or sliced cake. Nuts, mints, and bonbons add to the beauty of the table, as does the attractive food.

Rules are relaxed with small teas, which can be served almost anywhere, including the coffee table. You can prepare and refrigerate most tea foods in advance.

A British tea is more extravagant than its American counterpart, but is easily adapted. The menu includes items such as meat, fish, and cheese, plus bread, jam, and cake. A half inch of milk is poured into each cup before tea is added. Lemon and sugar are offered as alternatives. The seated hostess serves at the table's end.

How to set the table for an afternoon tea

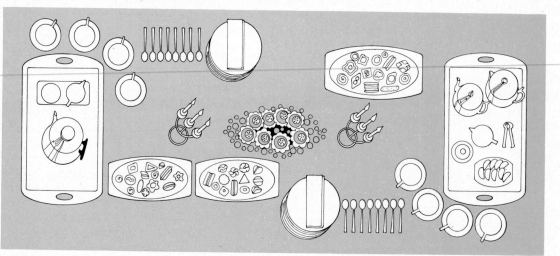

England, Ireland, Scotland, and Wales influenced the choice of table appointments above. The massive arrangement of garden flowers strengthens the British Isles decorating scheme, and complements the tea and light refreshments served in the authentic English tradition.

Informal Table Settings

Three times a day, 365 days a year, 1,095 times annually, meals can either be a dreadful bore or a boost to the entire family's morale. The choice is yours because you can put extra glamour into meals with an exciting table setting.

When it comes to informal table settings, the family should come first. A beautiful table produces better manners and conversation. A gracious table promotes sharing of ambitions and dreams during the one time everyone is there together. Dinner is the key meal, family breakfast second, and luncheon, especially on weekends, an important third. Setting the table carefully and beautifully for your family makes the transition to entertaining easy.

Because the rules for setting informal tables are few, you can exercise a great deal of initiative. However, remember that the comfort of your family or guests still reigns supreme. There are also a few other ideas that you may want to keep in mind when setting the table. For example, to make use of your tableware, try alternating the settings and place mats. Always arrange each place setting with the same care as if entertaining royalty. Or, recycle short, stubby candles by placing them into stubby holders. The children are often charmed with helping set the table, if allowed to add their own creativity.

Informal entertaining has never been as popular as now. Even truly elegant table settings can be informal in format. For serving a multitude, this style is best even if extra help is available. And, for the hostess who must plan the menu and prepare and serve the food, this kind of entertaining is practically painless.

Spring sets the theme of this casual country table setting. The provincial feeling of the centerpiece is echoed by figurines placed at each setting and by the easy-care cloth with contrasting check napkins. Mixing two kinds of dinnerware is very effective for luncheon.

Relaxed Sit-Down Dinners

When serving one of these dinners, keep the courses to a minimum. Use your living room for the serving of either dessert or the first course to avoid the problem of table clearing. Substitute hors d'oeuvres, including vegetables, even cold fish, for the usual appetizer. The main course and dessert served at the table then require only one change of service. Or, start with an appetizer and serve the main course, with the dessert to be served in the living room. Remember that cleanup problems undoubtedly will arise if more than one course is served in the living room.

Ice water prepoured, butter pats preplaced on bread-and-butter plates, and individual salads preset all give a festive look, and mean less last-minute work. If you plan an appetizer, put it in place before guests are invited to the table.

One-dish main courses can be served by the host from a casserole before him. In this case, stack the plates before him as well, with napkins centered in front of each guest. It is easiest if the host also serves the vegetables; otherwise, pass them. Remove everything germane to the main course before dessert is served. Either position the dessert at the time it is brought to the table or have the host serve it.

The simple order of things is maintained in each place setting. Position flatware in order of use, first items to the outside. Bread-and-butter plates keep crumbs off a table when place mats are used. If coffee is served with the meal, place the teaspoon on the saucer to the right of the handle. Dessert flatware can be placed directly on the dessert plates, if you wish.

A wheeled serving cart or a large tray is a great help for both dispensing and dispersing food. Another ideal accessory piece is a sideboard or buffet. The serving dishes can be arranged there, with the guests invited to help themselves and then be seated at the table.

For the table setting scheme, almost anything goes nowadays, just so long as it does not interfere in any way with the serving of the food. Straw place mats and stainless

Give the simplest meal an intriguing new slant. Ideal for small-space dining, a circular table is covered with two cloths that carry out the color scheme of your centerpiece and tableware. Alternate the points and use matching napkins.

steel flatware, colorful casual dinnerware, chunky footed tumblers, and an inventive centerpiece can set an inviting tone.

A floral arrangement is the natural choice for an elegant dinner. For more casual occasions, even every day, give the table a focus of interest by using objects found around the home. Or, arrange a basket of daisies and eggs as a conversation piece at a Sunday night soufflé supper. A blooming houseplant deserves its own hours of honor —and it can become the center of interest on the breakfast table. A dried arrangement of foliage, pods, and flowers can be used as an eye-catching centerpiece throughout the fall and winter months.

And don't forget that candles add to the festiveness of any dinner. They come in a variety of styles, sizes, shapes, and colors. Textured, squatty shapes are especially effective with a low centerpiece arrangement and casual dinnerware and flatware. Depending upon the shape of the centerpiece, tall tapers might be the best answer for you. The most important element of all is your own fun and ingenuity.

Almost oriental with its free-flowing lines, the earthenware dinnerware above has opaline blue, lavender, and green designs on a misty aqua background. It is durable enough for everyday use, beautiful enough for entertaining.

Traditional styles are mixed on the table above. The flatware is stainless, the candlesticks and napkin rings are pewter, and the blue goblets are of pressed glass. Blue Onion pattern china plates rest atop pewter trenches.

Casual Luncheons

Like male executives, many busy women find that a luncheon is a great time to get together. Since the hostess has to serve the food as well as participate in whatever is the important project to be discussed, the better her battle plan for serving, the easier the event will be for her.

Not all luncheons have such specific reasons for existence as gathering committee members or bridge partners. It is a fine time for any feminine gathering. On weekends, an informal luncheon often includes spouses as well.

For females only, choose the fare with your diet-conscious friends in mind, and generally be simple, dainty, and perhaps even fancy. This is all the more reason for emphasizing the environment; set your table in a way that makes even the weight-watchers feel well feasted.

The same basics apply to a luncheon as do with a dinner, except that traditionally, no candles are used before dusk. Spotless linens, gleaming flatware, and sparkling glassware are necessities for entertaining of this kind. If the tabletop is good-looking, reveal it with place mats instead of using a full tablecloth. Your best table finery can likewise be used for informal entertaining as a special honor to your guests.

Figurines or small, individual vases of flowers flanking the centerpiece can fill the space that ordinarily is taken by candles and candleholders, which you would use at a meal later in the day. If coffee or tea are to be served with the meal, make sure that each place setting is wide enough to accommodate a cup and saucer placed beside the plate.

For special party luncheons, make use of card tables for seating the diners. Set the dining table or buffet for self-serving. Maintain a cohesive decorating scheme by covering the card tables in coordinated cloths. They can be removed easily if the tables will be needed later for play. Mini-centerpieces are attractive on small tables, but they need to be removed later. A single flower at each guest's place setting, or an exotic napkin fold, might be decoration enough for your luncheon.

Offer iced tea, water, or iced coffee if the weather is warm. Place the iced-tea spoon to the outside of the conventional flatware setting on the right. Set all of these items on the table well before guests arrive.

An Aztec-inspired sunburst in hues of yellow, bittersweet, and charcoal brown decorates this dinnerware of fiery red. Because it is durable and dishwasher, detergent, and oven safe, it is ideal for serving both family and guests.

The octagonal plate above with its bittersweet flower and vine motif blends beautifully with rooms that have a Shaker touch. The pistol-handled flatware and the pewter chalice are apt partners in the simple setting.

Hearty Weekend Brunches

Holidays and weekends find many hostesses planning eye-opening brunches. Midmorning is the right time for this happy blending of breakfast and lunch. Late sleepers can rouse themselves for the appointed hour of eleven, although ten can be picked if the meal is to precede an early afternoon event. Allow for flexibility in scheduling Sunday brunches so that your guests can go to church.

Greet the guests with a thirst-quenching beverage as soon as they arrive. Have coffee ready for those who scorn juice. Have non-alcoholic alternatives if you are offering alcoholic beverages.

An elaborate brunch includes many dishes, served smorgasbord fashion, both hot and cold. Simpler fare includes a main hot dish, usually egg-based, with plenty of breakfast pastry. In either case, a good serving piece to keep warmed foods hot is the major feature of the table. This is the perfect time to use a chafing dish, warming tray, or one of the miraculous new electric tabletop appliances. Use your supersize coffeepot as well, or put every coffeepot in the house to work.

Brunches are almost always served buffet style, with help-yourself seconds for eager eaters. Plan a backyard brunch in the spring or fall as a welcome surprise. The casualness of the occasion means that many guests can be invited. The menu can usually be managed with low cost.

If you plan a sit-down brunch on a weekend or holiday morning, make it as colorful as possible. Use a tablecloth, place mats, or table runners in colors that harmonize with the dinnerware and centerpiece.

It is always a good idea to coordinate colors to flatter food, but especially so for the first meal of the day. With egg dishes, consider reds, oranges, and browns in winter. Whites and pastels would flatter such food for spring or summer.

Elegant appointments are in order if the brunch is to celebrate an auspicious occasion, such as a wedding breakfast, engagement announcement, or a christening.

Conversely, country casual suits a pre-football game gathering or a hike through the countryside. If no special event has been planned for after the brunch, be prepared to have the guests linger well into the afternoon. Just as company arrives at staggered times, so does it depart.

Breakfasts for a Better Day

Too often, breakfast is a harried meal with little or no grace. There is nothing nicer than starting the day with a meal that is pleasantly presented. An inviting breakfast table setting gives the soul sustenance all through the day. It will help ensure that the family starts with their best foot forward, amply fortified.

Nutritionists emphasize the importance of a healthy breakfast. A midmorning lag interferes with anyone's activities, especially school-age children. Picky eaters in particular need the extra coaxing that attractive presentation can give to that first meal. Eager earlybirds can take a few extra moments to make the table attractive. Night

Year-round cheerfulness abounds in this colorful breakfast room setting. The centerpiece of stacked lemons and the white and yellow plastic dinnerware fit the mood of the contemporary design pedestal table and chairs.

owls can use the last few minutes at night to set the table. Having the coffeepot filled and ready for plugging in makes morning copable.

Another idea that can help you get a jump on fixing breakfasts is having condiments such as jams and jellies, sugar, salt, and pepper permanently displayed on the table. Or, give some thought to decanting these into attractive containers and centering them on a mat or tray.

Having company for breakfast is sometimes the order of the day. For example, overnight guests need to be fed, but they might find a brunch too time-wasting. Inviting a friend's weekend guests over for breakfast the day she plans a party will endear you to her forever. Moving day morning is another time when any woman would be delighted to have you manage breakfast for her brood.

A breakfast invitation is welcome when a new baby's arrival takes the mother away from home. Wives of crack-of-dawn golfers or hunters can share the breakfast burden by alternating their invitations to the men. It is from such humble beginnings that truly gracious hostessing starts.

Breakfast differs from any other meal. Hot foods are served directly onto individual plates and placed directly before the diners. As soon as he or she is served, the diner should eat without waiting for the hostess to be seated. If fresh fruit is served as an appetizer, allow sufficient time before beginning the hot foods so that it can be comfortably eaten.

Serve fruit juice either centered on a plate or above the knife on the right. Arrange breakfast flatware in order of use from the outside in; dinner fork on the left, knife to the right of the plate, cereal spoon to its right, and a teaspoon for fruit (but not for coffee) to its right. A butter spreader goes across the top of the bread-and-butter plate. To avoid confusion, it is best to eliminate any flatware that is not necessary for a specific breakfast menu.

Coffee cups go to the right of the plate, with the spoons to the right of the cup. Alternately, they can be stacked near the hostess for filling and passing.

This counter breakfast setting is colorful, but uncluttered. The blue and white checked place mats match the chair seats and repeat the blue in the wall tiles. A single pot of yellow mums adds a touch of sparkling contrast.

Red warms up this breakfast setting, and provides a sharp contrast to the expanse of greenery outside. The lovely red tureen echoes the red trim on the window shade, and the abundant bowl of fruit adds a myriad of colors.

For regular family breakfasts, almost any kind of linen may be used. Many breakfast tables are pretty enough to be left exposed. Paper napkins may also rule the waking house. A distinctive color will help cheer up any table setting.

A wardrobe of place mats for informal breakfasting can create multiple effects. Mix them as well as using them matched. Try the new disposable ones.

Why not treat the family as company for weekend breakfasts? If place mats have been the rule for everyday use, achieve instant effect with a tablecloth. Substitute stemware for tumblers to serve juice. Try a fancy napkin fold with a cloth napkin for a change. Liberate your elegant luncheon plates for the occasion, too.

Long, lingering, luxurious breakfasts can be shared with the family when electric appliances such as frypans are used at the table. If Dad is the traditional weekend breakfast chef, his efforts definitely deserve special stage setting.

Weekends are ideal times to experiment with new breakfast ideas. Preparing and serving breakfasts that are traditional to other lands and other parts of the United States will take everyone by surprise. For example, if a substantial Sunday midday meal is planned, a petit déjeuner might be just right. Or, for something fancifully French, use a red and white checked tablecloth, blue napkins in red napkin rings, and a bouquet of peonies.

Consider serving breakfast in another room of the house now and then. Serve foods that need little cutting and that can be handled easily on a coffee table or a snack tray. A roaring fireplace is an ideal foil for a winter weekend breakfast. A dew-softened summer lawn is an inviting backdrop for a light summer repast.

The ultimate location of luxury is the proverbial breakfast in bed. When someone is sick, it becomes a necessity. Flagging spirits are instantly raised with a cheery breakfast tray. If you do not own a footed tray, use stacked books on either side to support a large tray for a sick child.

A cloth covering for a tray is not only pretty, it helps anchor the dishes. Warm the plates in advance. Use an upended soup bowl as a warmer to make sure food arrives hot. Or, cover the food with aluminum foil. Disguise a vacuum bottle beneath a draped napkin. Decorate the tray with a mini-flower arrangement.

Breakfast, the unsung hero meal that gets us all going, needs special care and consideration. With a little effort, you can make it both bright-eyed and beautiful!

24

Buffet Meals

The casual tone of an informal buffet meal is warm and inviting, which generally puts guests at ease. For the hostess and/or host, it is self-serving in more ways than one. Buffet-style is the easiest way to serve a large number of guests nicely. One great advantage of this kind of entertaining is that the one who is entertaining is free to mingle with the guests and enjoy the party, too. Guests help themselves, so there's no problem with serving, and the only concern is with replenishing the buffet serving dishes. Do most of the work of preparing a buffet well in advance.

Any meal can be served buffet-style, so long as the food served lends itself to long-term warming and can be managed on a plate easily. Buffet brunches are weekend favorites in many homes.

Cocktail party buffets are preferred by many for the holiday season. Potluck suppers, where each woman brings her own food specialty, demand an elegantly set table as background. A late-night buffet after a movie or the theater is universally considered the critic's choice.

Seek out the various locations in your home that lend themselves to buffet setups, in addition to the dining table or sideboard. Possibilities include the family room, den, attic, garage, and even the kitchen. For a large party, you should set more than one buffet table to be sure that no hungry guest is kept waiting. A new location for any buffet table opens up fresh possibilities for tabletop decor, and can prove to be more convenient.

The same rules of convenience apply to an informal buffet table as for more formal settings. Plan the table progression with

The festive buffet table below shows off a fresh color plan—red, white, green, and grape. The bold patterned table cover features motifs of stylized grapes. The same exotic grape color is repeated in the plates, napkins, servers, and salt and pepper shakers.

plates first, main course next, space next to serving dishes so that plates may be set down, and beverages either last or served from a separate tray.

The placement of the table itself is important, especially for a large party. Keep it away from the seating area so that those who are getting seconds will not disturb those who are eating. Latecomers will not create a traffic snarl if the table is kept away from the entrance hall. Make sure there is no bottleneck between those waiting to serve themselves and the guests who have already filled their plates. Avoid these and other hazards by checking the line-up before your meal gets underway.

Choose strong table decorations, both in color and character, for a buffet table. The first impression is what counts, for this is not a table one lingers over. Flowers are always nicest when they emphasize the detailing of the dinnerware used. Use a cluster of candles, a bouquet of dried weeds, or any attractive object to give the table a center of interest. Just make sure it is color coordinated and in scale with the other tabletop items.

Informal tablecloths run the gamut from colorful linens to printed paper. Pick patterns from fabric remnants to make a floor-length cloth. Or, use a patterned permanent-press sheet to make a table cover. The 15-inch drop is not mandatory, but it makes a table more elegant. Cloths can be used together to gain length. A small table works best with a wildly printed cloth and no centerpiece at all. Nice but not necessary is an extra cloth to cover up any spills before dessert is served.

Other niceties include individual trays or snack trays for your guests. Extra-large napkins are handy for all, particularly youngsters. A tea cart is a real boon for clearing and refilling the main dishes or for holding dessert and coffee.

Most hollow ware is multipurpose, so use it inventively. Gravy boats can hold any sauces, celery, or mounded cherry tomatoes. A chip and dip tray can hold rolls, with whipped butter in the center dip bowl.

A salt shaker will also dispense powdered sugar for berries. Silver trays can hold ham

The white dinnerware, black napkins, and splashy yellow mums reiterate the colors in this patterned tablecloth. Brass and gold tones accent the setting with their gleam. Purple iris, used sparingly with the mums, provide contrast.

or turkey, if it is already sliced. Casual settings can include foil-lined baskets or decorated paper paint buckets to hold salads, rolls, and breads.

Disposable plastic and paper plates, and cups are both pretty and practical. However, owning a special matched buffet set of colorful, inexpensive dinnerware and flatware is a good long-term investment.

Mixing and matching tableware is perfectly fine if everyday sets are selected with an eye to coordinating them with more formal sets. Use your judgment in deciding whether or not sets of dinnerware or flatware look well together. Why not set a two-sided buffet with different sets on each side? Alternate mixed flatware place settings on two napkin colors, or arrange them into two different groupings. Anything goes, so long as it is pretty.

Dining in the Great Outdoors

The sky is the limit for dining locations outdoors. Use the backyard and porch, and expand your dining horizons to include breakfast on a balcony, cookouts in a park, a boathouse brunch, or a picnic in a stadium parking lot before the big game.

Tables need plenty of character to match the expanse of the great outdoors. Most meals are casual, with relaxed manners for eating corn on the cob and hand-held hot dogs. Use strong, bright colors to spotlight the table and make it up-beat.

Use table decorations that reflect the occasion or the meal itself—cork floats for a fish fry, Mexican decorations for a barbecue, party favors for a birthday, or mock firecrackers for the Fourth of July. An easy source for a centerpiece is the garden. Select from the abundant fruits and vegetables of the season.

A well-groomed garden or a patio is a wonderful background for an elegant table setting. Crystal stemware and silver flatware and serving pieces take on a wonderful gleam at twilight or when they are surrounded by the glow of candles at night.

The rules of comfort apply to outdoor table settings just as they would to indoor ones. However, there are some other special considerations as well.

First and foremost, plan an alternate location in the event of inclement weather, or make a rain-check date, since weather is a vital factor. Protect your place settings against dust with a cloth or paper if you set them well in advance. Try to avoid windy corners. Also keep in mind that direct sun can be nice in the spring or fall, but it can be insufferable in the middle of the summer. Falling leaves or blossoms are always unwelcome table guests, so make sure that you don't place your table where it's bound to collect them.

Use napkin rings to anchor paper napkins and to dress up cloth ones. Colorful paperweights or even shiny rocks can be used on napkins or to hold the table cover at each corner. Another trick is to sew elastic diagonally across the underneath corners of the cloth so that it can slip under each corner of the table.

Candles will need protection from breezes. Choose those in glass containers, or buy elegant chimneys to use with fine

This striking luncheon setting gets its inspiration from the flowers on the patio, with yellow dominating the scene. The yellow and white tabletop appointments are ideally suited to the strong print of the cloth.

An informal fish fry launched this decorative theme. Bright enamelware place settings rest on a fish-skin motif vinyl table cover. A tall arrangement of daisies, placed at the end of the table, doesn't hinder conversation.

Whimsical piglet place mats might set the stage the next time you stage a barbecue. Small piglets of twisted yarn tie the napkins, and a spring arrangement of daisies and globe amaranth decorates the table. For a real country touch, add a wicker pig as a table decoration.

candleholders. Votive-type candles at each setting are charming and functional. Use lots of candles to properly light the food.

Flambeau lights (wicks saturated with a quick-burning fuel on a tall pole) are good additional outdoor lights. Consider hanging miniature white Christmas lights in trees. Try some regular outdoor lights tucked inside paper lanterns. At the shore, fill big brown bags halfway with sand, plant a candle in the center of each one, and place the candles somewhere near the dining area. A candlelit front walk is a perfect party starter.

Create a separate cookout corner for the chef, and make sure that the dining area is not downwind. Decorate the chef's table, and be sure he has some trays handy. Use waterproof pillows or bright towels to provide additional buffet-style seating. Decorate a trash can for used paper plates and other disposable items.

For picnics, good thermal containers are a must. Lightweight paper or plastic plates are easiest to carry. Regular flatware is worth its weight in convenience. Take along a supersized cloth or brightly patterned sheet, and guests can sit on its edges. You will need loads of napkins, either colored paper or more elegant cloth. Stick to squatty tumblers and serving pieces that stay upright on uneven surfaces.

Atmosphere and Lighting

Creating the most attractive atmosphere for dining takes consideration of every element in the room. The table decorations themselves set the theme and make the biggest contribution to the mood. But the background environment plays a part that is almost equally important.

In decorating a dining area, choose colors that flatter your table appointments. Chances are that your dinnerware and glassware colors are favorites that you would choose for other elements anyway. The colors need not be the same, but they should be in keeping with the appointments.

Pastels flatter formal table appointments and give a feeling of serenity. They make a room seem more spacious; consequently, they are ideal choices for small dining areas. A wall covered with mirrors or a mural can also be a room expander. Bright, cheerful colors make a room seem smaller and more intimate. They are often chosen, as are earth tones, for kitchen or breakfast nook areas. Usually, cool colors such as lavender, blue, and green are less flattering to food than warm colors such as red, yellow, and orange.

Subdued patterns and textures are most suitable for traditional table schemes. Use elegant material such as velvet, tapestry, brocade, or satin to suit these furnishings best. Multicolored pastel florals and stripes are often chosen for chair coverings and wall coverings with traditional tables. The same choice might seem dull in contrast to a sharply contrasting, roughly textured contemporary table. A neutral background allows the most table changes.

← The play of colors and textures in the dining room at the left is as pleasant to the eye as good food is to the palate. The autumn colors in the centerpiece repeat the color of the furnishings, and the lighting fixture above casts a tranquil note over the entire setting.

If your dining area has a definite color scheme or furniture style, make every effort to match your table setting to it.

Lighting is also a major factor in setting the mood of a dining area. Lighting should flatter the diners as well as the food. Warm lights instead of fluorescent ones accomplish this best. Candlelight is the most flattering of all lighting.

Try to avoid having dark, lightless areas surrounding the table because contrasts are fatiguing. A relatively equal field of light throughout the entire dining area is generally your best bet. Accessory furniture gains drama with the use of accent lights. All lighting should be kept soft, even the lighting away from the table.

Check the lighting from each person's seat to make sure that there are no unpleasant glares either on or off the table. Windows present different lighting at various times of the day and of the year, so make this check frequently. A lovely spill of light from a picture window might be too strong in midsummer, or with reflections from sun-drenched snow.

Because table lighting is so very important, consider it first, then adjust the lighting in the rest of the room. If you have a dimmer switch in the dining area, you can easily control the overhead lights and chandeliers. Compensate for added candlelight by lowering the other lights.

Overhead table lights always should be above eye level and soft enough so as to prevent glare, whereas candles should be either above or below eye level. Locate lights so that no sharp shadows distort the design of your dining table.

Buffet tables need plenty of lighting to ensure that guests can see what they are serving themselves. It sets the table apart from the room and makes it dramatic. Remember that dark cloths absorb light, so they need more light than do light cloths. Your table is your stage; direct the lighting so that your setting is a scene stealer.

How to Select Your Tableware

Tableware should be selected, collected, treasured, and used. Even though you've probably never painted a canvas with oils or created a piece of sculpture, you can easily acquire the fundamentals of design and color, plus a broad knowledge of the many different types of dinnerware. Use the same care in selecting tableware that you would use in assembling a wardrobe.

Nowadays, more people travel to faraway places, see and do more, and get involved in new experiences. And, their impressions are reflected in their homes. Regardless of whether you want to inject a bit of excitement, serenity, or nostalgia into your daily routine, there's no simpler way to do this than by selecting table settings that convey the particular mood that you desire.

← This festive buffet features well-coordinated table settings—the china, flatware, stemware, and serving pieces are all enhanced by the lively flowered tablecloth and lace-edged napkins.

Homemakers are constantly searching for more imaginative designs in tableware, and this has inspired a burst of creativity from tabletop designers to fill these needs.

Selecting tableware should involve more than taking one trip through your favorite tableware department. After all, choosing something that will play a vital role in your home for years is an all-important decision.

Also browse through shops that display total tabletop ideas—tables covered with cloths, mats, or runners and topped with dinnerware, flatware, crystal, centerpieces, napkins, and napkin rings. Note how the professional designers combine the latest in table settings. Experiment a little on your own, too. The sales person will be happy to help you assemble pieces so you can see how they look together. Combine different types of dinnerware and flatware. Then, arrange them on a table with a colorful cover, and add a centerpiece.

Just keep in mind that if the designs are artistically good, not merely a whim of fashion, they will still be appealing after many years.

How to Select Dinnerware

Dinnerware is the single word that encompasses that wide, wide, wonderful world of china, stoneware, pottery, and plastic. And selecting dinnerware can be as exciting for the homemaker of many years who wants to add new life to her long-used table settings as it is for the bride-to-be who is furnishing her first home.

There's no doubt about it: selecting dinnerware is a matter of personal taste; but it must be governed by your budget, too. Also, your choice will depend on your life-style, the type of entertaining you do, and the number of family members.

Many people still feel that dinnerware needs consist of one set of dishes in fine china for special occasions, and another in a less formal pattern for everyday. However, don't feel that you have to pledge your allegiance to this plan.

With more and more emphasis being placed on informal and casual table settings, you can combine patterns and different types of dinnerware. And when you are buying your dinnerware, think of flexibility instead of quantity. You'll have much more fun setting your table with a variety of go-together patterns than you will with a large service in an unimaginative 'safe' pattern.

Whether you lean toward the bold designs of modern interpretations, the designs and colors that take their cue from nature, or the traditional designs that are a part of this era of nostalgia, you will find that manufacturers and designers have anticipated your desires. The selection of dinnerware in all types, designs, colors, and prices is greater than ever before.

When you select your dinnerware, you know that you want it to be beautiful, in good taste, long-lasting, and functional, but there are also some other considerations.

1. Cups should be shaped so they are not easily tippable, and the handles should be large enough so they are easy to grasp. The cup should fit firmly in the saucer.

2. Plates that are round are easier to stack than square or free-form ones.

3. Heavily embossed patterns collect dust and food in the grooves and may need to be cleaned frequently with a brush.

4. Most dinnerware, both casual and good china, is sold by the single place setting as well as by the individual piece. However, there is usually a price advantage if you buy four, six, eight, or twelve place settings. Also, a few serving pieces are usually included when you buy a whole set.

The drawings below show the more popular pieces of dinnerware from which to select place settings: A. dinner plate; B. salad plate; C. bread-and-butter plate; D. soup bowl; E. oval baker; F. cup and saucer; G. cereal bowl; H. mug; I. egg cup; and J. fruit dish.

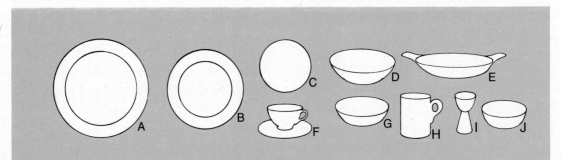

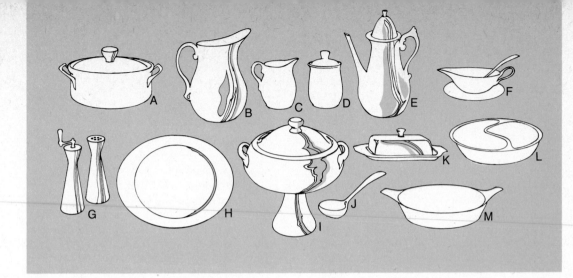

The drawings above show an assortment of dinnerware serving pieces from which to choose: A. casserole; B. pitcher; C. creamer; D. sugar bowl; E. coffeepot; F. gravy server; G. salt and pepper shaker; H. platter; I. tureen; J. ladle; K. covered butter dish; L. vegetable dish; and M. oval baker. You can add these one at a time as your budget allows.

Dictionary of Dinnerware

There are so many different types of dinnerware available that it is helpful to be able to distinguish among them.

1. Ceramic includes any articles made of so-called earth materials such as sand, clay, etc., that are processed by firing or baking. This classification includes pottery, earthenware, china, and glass.

2. Earthenware dinnerware is made from more refined clays than is pottery, with other ingredients added to give it a whiter body. Like pottery, it is fired at a relatively low temperature, and it is opaque and porous. It is much more resistant to chipping or breakage than is pottery dinnerware.

3. Fine earthenware is a type of soft, white ware that is fired at higher temperatures than the others. One example is ironstone, which is a heavy, durable earthenware. Ironstone is sometimes confused with stoneware or semivitreous china.

4. Stoneware is a hard ware made of a single light clay and fired at a high temperature. It is nonporous and very durable, but it usually has a slightly gray cast.

5. Semivitrified or semiporcelain is a type of dinnerware about halfway between china and earthenware in body composition, firing temperatures, and durability.

6. Ovenware is clayware that is able to withstand the heat of a kitchen oven without damage, permitting the homemaker to prepare oven-cooked food in it and then to use it for table service. Ovenware is usually casual in design and features bright colors.

7. China is a nonporous, nonabsorbent type of clayware made of special white clay and fired at exceptionally high temperatures. The finer grades are generally thin, translucent, resistant to chipping, and will ring clearly when tapped.

8. Porcelain is a hard, translucent clayware body that differs from china only in the manufacturing process. In all other respects, the two are so similar that the terms are generally used interchangeably.

9. Bone china has all the desirable qualities of fine china, but it has a minimum of 25 percent bone ash in its composition to give it a stark white color.

10. Fine china is made of choice refined clays that are fired at a temperature high enough to make the clay particles melt and fuse. The result is a completely nonporous, acid-resistant dinnerware. Generally, it is rich off-white or ivory in color.

11. Melamine is the chemical name for the compound from which most plastic dinnerware is made. It is nonporous, nonabsorbent, and break and chip resistant.

How to Select Flatware

Even if you are selecting a silver baby spoon and fork for a gift for a new baby, you realize that buying flatware represents a substantial investment in both time and money. And, when you are shopping for flatware for your own use, it becomes even more important that you select it wisely.

It's up to you to protect your investment by acquiring a knowledge of what silver is, how and from where to select it, and how to use it and care for it. Also, use your ingenuity in selecting flatware so that it harmonizes with your dinnerware, crystal, and table linens.

Whether it's a hurry-up breakfast for your own family members or a formal sit-down dinner for guests, your flatware can create a gracious and hospitable mood.

Depending upon your style of living and/or your budget, you have a choice of sterling, silverplate, gold electroplate, or stainless steel. Your selection should reflect both your creativity and efficiency and make dining a pleasure.

Sterling Silver

There's no denying that sterling is the 'Rolls Royce' of flatware. Because sterling is solid silver, its quality regulated by law, it will last for generations. The more you use it, the lovelier it becomes. Frequent use prevents tarnish and helps to develop a satiny luster—a patina appreciated by admirers of good silver. Sterling will never go out of style, and it can be passed on to your grandchildren.

You may wonder why sterling prices vary when it is all made of solid silver. This is because of the difference there is in designs, weight, and craftsmanship.

Silverplate

Less expensive than sterling, but with equally as many patterns to choose from, silverplated flatware is a favorite with many homemakers. There are many different prices and qualities, but the better brands have a base metal of nickel silver (an alloy of copper, nickel, and zinc).

The higher-priced silverplate looks and feels like sterling, and is heavy and perfectly balanced. Besides the overall plating, the most-used items such as spoons and forks have an overlay of pure silver plated on the areas of greatest wear.

Gold Electroplate

For those who are seeking a flatware service that is elegantly different and in impeccably good taste, gold electroplate has special appeal. Many people prefer gold electroplate because it is both reasonable in price and easy to maintain.

Fine quality gold-electroplated flatware is about the same price as a comparable quality of silverplate. It is long-lasting, will never tarnish, needs no polishing, and is dishwasher safe.

Stainless

It took several years for stainless steel flatware to venture out of the kitchen. In its infancy, it was regarded as a cheap substitute for good silver, and was regarded as 'everyday' flatware.

This modern metal—a combination of steel, chrome, and nickel—is a favorite with gifted silversmiths who concentrate on producing patterns that are as beautiful as those in sterling, silverplate, and gold electroplate. It's no wonder that many of today's homemakers choose stainless for everyday use and for guests.

Be sure to purchase your flatware from a reliable dealer. Then, you can be sure that it is of accepted quality and made by a manufacturer of integrity.

You're bound to find several, or even many patterns that please you in each of the types of flatware that are available.

Compare them side by side to narrow down the choice. Then, arrange them as you would on your own table, and ask yourself the following questions about them:

1. Does the pattern have a beauty that promises to endure—not only for today, but for many years to come?

2. When you arrange a place setting, do the pieces remain flat on the table? They should not wobble around.

3. Is the pattern that you have selected still appealing to you when you arrange four, six, or eight place settings? A pattern that you may like individually may become quite monotonous when it is repeated around the dining table.

4. Is the structural design such that each piece is suited to its job? Is there proportion, harmony, and balance?

5. Take notice of the distribution of weight of flatware. Is the greatest amount of weight and thickness in the handle and points that will receive the most pressure? The knife should not be heavy, and the fork should taper from each end toward a point of maximum thickness at the narrowest part of the handle.

6. Does each piece in the flatware set have maximum utility?

7. Is the bowl of the spoon in proportion to the handle? You can find out by balancing the spoon.

8. Is the knife easy to hold? The handle should provide ample room for the hand, and the blade should be thick and balanced to provide comfort for the index finger.

The next step in flatware selection is to decide just what pieces to collect first. It's always wise to be practical and get the basic place settings first. The basic four-piece place setting consists of a place knife, place fork, teaspoon, and salad fork. The five-piece place setting has a cream-soup or place spoon in addition to the four pieces. The six-piece setting has a butter spreader added to the five-piece place setting.

After you've decided on the size you like, buy as many place settings as you can afford. You can always add more gradually. And, as time goes on, you may want to supplement your place units with additional pieces such as iced beverage and demitasse spoons, cocktail forks, and an assortment of serving pieces.

The drawings below represent the various pieces that are available in flatware place settings. Start with the basics first.

There are many serving pieces you can add to your collection of flatware. These do not have to be the same pattern as your place settings.

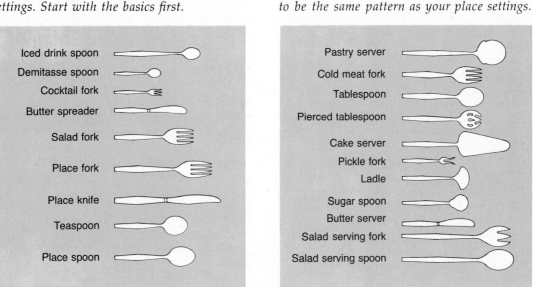

Iced drink spoon	Pastry server
Demitasse spoon	Cold meat fork
Cocktail fork	Tablespoon
Butter spreader	Pierced tablespoon
Salad fork	Cake server
Place fork	Pickle fork
Place knife	Ladle
Teaspoon	Sugar spoon
Place spoon	Butter server
	Salad serving fork
	Salad serving spoon

Selecting Stemware and Glassware

When you choose your stemware and glassware, remember that you want it to be beautiful and functional. You also want it to enhance your dinnerware, flatware, and room decor. Everything else in your place setting rests flat on the table, but glassware adds another dimension—height. The sparkle of the polished glass makes whatever you serve seem more elegant, and it captures sunlight, candlelight, or the light from the chandelier.

When you are shopping for stemware, watch for graceful proportions. Even though you may be more attracted to pattern or color, or adaptability to your needs, remember that the shape, in terms of symmetry, has a vital place in the artistry of glassware. Stemmed goblets, for example, add a graceful note to the table, but they can also be a hazard if they tip easily. Be sure to check the base for proportionate breadth and weight before you make your selection.

If you're purchasing stemware a piece at a time, start with the water goblets first, then add sherbets, then the wines.

Crystal

The word 'crystal' stems from early efforts by craftsmen to duplicate rock crystal. True crystal has a high percentage of lead content, and is made from highly refined materials. It is hand-blown, hand-cut, and hand-polished. It has a beauty that resembles a fine diamond.

Here are some of the ways you can determine the quality of crystal:

1. Look for the unmistakable sheen and brilliance not found in ordinary glassware.

2. Clear crystal should never have the slightest muddy or off-color to it.

3. Colored stemware should have a deep and rich sparkling luster.

4. Listen for a bell-like tone when you tap the rim of a goblet with your fingernail, while holding the footed base. It's the ring of strength and lasting brilliancy.

5. Be sure that the edges are perfectly smooth and that there are no scratches or bumps. These are the result of insufficient polishing. The glass should appear to be entirely free from waves or bubbles.

Pressed Glass

Just as the name implies, pressed glass is made by pressing molten glass—either by hand or by machine—into a mold that has a previously designed pattern. It contains lime for greater strength and workability.

Pressed glass is not as brilliant as lead glass, nor does it have the same ring.

Because it is heavier and more rugged than other glassware, pressed glass is an ideal choice for informal table settings—ironstone, pottery, or plastic. Its durability makes it perfect for patio meals and for children's use. While no glassware is impervious to breakage, it does stand a better chance of surviving rough usage. There's even less chance of breakage if you choose your pressed glassware in one of the unfooted or tumbler styles.

It comes in an array of beautiful colors, too. You can mix the colors of amethyst, ruby, amber, blue, and green according to the seasons, the dinnerware you plan to use it with, and your decor.

Milk Glass

Milk glass is a distinctive kind of glassware, and is especially popular with those who favor Early American furnishings in their homes. It is easily distinguished by its opaque, milk-white color.

Glassware Decorations

It's up to you to decide whether you want glassware that has a classic and simple design or one that is richly ornate. In either case, it's well to understand the glassware decorating processes.

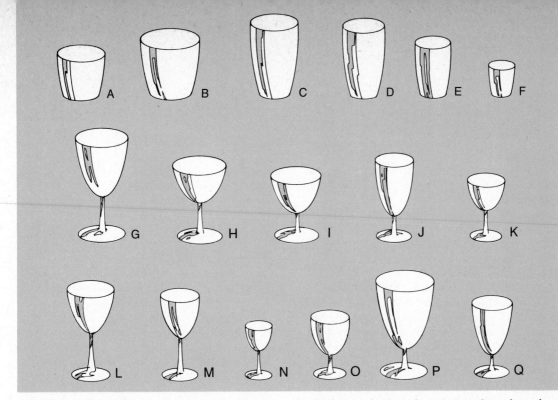

The illustrations above represent the popular sizes of stemware and glassware: A. 7½ oz. old-fashioned cocktail; B. 12 oz. double old-fashioned or other tall drinks; C. 12 oz. highball; D. 9 oz. scotch and soda; E. 5 oz. whiskey sour or other short cocktail; F. 1½ oz. jigger (whiskey); G. 10 oz. all-purpose goblet; H. 9 oz. sherbet and wine glass; I. 7 to 8 oz. low sherbet and wine glass; J. 6 oz. whiskey-sour glass; K. 4 oz. cocktail glass; L. 5 oz. claret glass; M. 4 oz. wine (white) or brandy glass; N. 1 oz. cordial for liqueurs; O. 4½ oz. sherry glass; P. 15 oz. luncheon goblet; and Q. 5 oz. orange juice or liqueur glass.

Cutting and etching are two of the most exquisite techniques for glass design. Cut glass cannot be surpassed in delicate light reflections. It is decorated by cutting patterns or figures into the surface.

Because it is highly susceptible to extreme heat or cold, it is most often found in heavy dishes such as bowls, bottles, and relish and candy dishes.

Etched glass appears to have an extremely fragile look because of its intricate tracery of fine line and its lacy design. Actually, it is more durable than cut glass, which has deeper grooves.

Platinum or gold bands on glassware are fired decorations. The name comes from the heating process necessary before the colored 'paints' become fused to the glass.

This design has a particular elegance, especially with the more-formal table settings. Use it to complement gold- or platinum-banded china, or dinnerware with gold or platinum designs. The accent at the top of the goblet makes it appear taller. Follow through in the rest of your table setting with matching tall tapers and a centerpiece in a similarly banded bowl.

Now that you've read about the various aspects of glassware—how it's manufactured, how it's decorated, and the types from which to choose, it's up to you to make your own selection. If your budget is limited, you may decide to purchase one piece at a time as you can afford it, or you may prefer to buy a complete set of very inexpensive glassware that can be replaced later on.

As with dinnerware and flatware, it is desirable to have two sets of glassware—one formal and one informal. The formal set will be stemware, and the informal set either tumblers or footed tumblers.

How to Select Table Linens

The creative use of table coverings affords you the opportunity to change your table scenery from one theme to another that is completely different. In order to do this, you'll need a basic supply of table coverings. This should include a variety of easy-care place mats for everyday use and several tablecloths that can be used for both formal and informal entertaining.

If you entertain frequently and enjoy giving your table settings personal flavor, you'll probably want a wide selection of colors, patterns, and materials in cloths, mats, runners, and napkins.

When you're shopping for table covers, look for the fiber content. The 'hang' tags on table covers and napkins should list the contents. This determines the price, the amount of wear you can expect, and what care you need to give them.

It's also a good idea to find out whether designs are applied by hand or machine. This will give you a clue as to the accuracy of the price. Roller-printed cloths are printed in volume, much like newspapers, while hand-blocked ones are printed singly.

Tablecloths

Before you start shopping for tablecloths, be sure to measure the size of your table. This is very important in selecting the right cloth. If you are buying a formal tablecloth, add 16 to 24 inches to both the length and width of the table for the drop. An informal cloth needs less drop—usually 10 to 14 inches. Never buy a cloth with less than 10 inches drop. The only kind of tablecloth that should touch the floor is a banquet cloth.

Hems should be narrow, with even, straight stitches. Hand-sewn hems are more handsome than machine-stitched hems.

Check on how much sizing is in a cloth. Do this by rubbing the folds of the cloth together. If this lessens the firmness, there's too much sizing and the cloth will lose its body after laundering. Too much sizing can be misleading, too, in regard to the cloth's weight and texture.

Place Mats

Place mats should be large enough to hold the entire place setting, but they should never overlap. Mats range in size from 12 to 14 inches deep and 16 to 18 inches wide.

Because they come in such a wide range of colors, designs, materials, sizes, and shapes, they are the most versatile of all table covers. You can find them in plastics, handwoven fibers and straws, cottons, linens, and silks. They are acceptable for every occasion except the most formal dinner table or a tea table.

Table Runners

A comparative newcomer to the tabletop scene, is the table runner. You can find them in the same wide variety of fabrics and synthetics as other table covers. Usually, runners are placed on either side of the table to hold numerous place settings, or they may be crisscrossed for four place settings. It's easy to get the exact length you need for your table, as you can purchase runner fabric by the yard.

Napkins

Napkins are often sold with tablecloths or place mats, but you can buy them separately. Napkins come in a variety of sizes. Dinner napkins are 18, 20, 22, or 24 inches square. 'Lapkins,' a favorite with men at buffet dinners, are 12 by 18 inches. Luncheon and breakfast napkins are 17 inches square. Tea napkins are 12 inches square, and cocktail napkins are either 4 by 6 inches or 6 by 8 inches. Paper napkins are widely used for everyday meals and for brunches and informal luncheons. Most cloth napkins are available in permanent-press fabrics.

How to Select Napkin Rings

At one time, and this was not too many years ago, it was the custom for everyone in the family to have his or her own napkin ring. These were usually made of sterling silver, or they were silver-plated. A monogrammed napkin ring was considered a very special gift to give to a new baby or a small child, just as much so as a baby spoon and fork. And, a pair of napkin rings, thoughtfully selected, was an appropriate wedding gift to present to a bride and groom.

As it became less and less common to use cloth napkins, except for very special occasions, napkin rings virtually disappeared from the table setting scene.

In the photo below, there are napkin rings for every type of table setting. Except for the silver ring, which you would buy in a flatware department, the others can be found in linen and giftware departments and shops.

Now that cloth napkins are being used much more widely than they have been for years (because of their easy-care permanent-press quality), napkin rings have reappeared. They are now, as they once were, a vital part of table settings. Another reason for their current widespread popularity is that there are so many designs, colors, and materials to choose from.

There are napkin rings to complement every type of table linen, dinnerware, flatware, and centerpiece. And, they are very reasonably priced—even the silver and gold napkin rings that you would use with elegant formal dinnerware are not as costly as you might think. Many novelty napkin rings that you would use for informal meals cost less than a dollar each.

For use with the casual types of earthenware, stoneware dinnerware, and colorful table linens, you can take your pick of napkin rings of many materials in a myriad of novel designs. There are wood napkin rings in either painted or natural finishes in round, oval, triangular, or square shapes. There are many that are handwoven of raffia. Very simple in design, but effective with the right table setting are the napkin rings that are merely a single strand of beads strung on a wire hoop.

To enhance a table set with contemporary dinnerware, choose napkin rings made of molded opaque plastic in a rainbow of colors. And to add a shimmering effect to a table setting, there's nothing like sparkling crystal-clear plastic napkin rings.

When you use your best silver or gold flatware and china, you will undoubtedly use matching silver or gold napkin rings.

If you're in doubt as to what napkin rings are best for you, take one each of your different napkins along with you when you shop. As you look over the assortment on display, try them on your napkins and you will have a good idea of whether they will be attractive. Keep adding until you have several sets to change with.

How to Make Table Linens

When you make your own table linens, you have unlimited possibilities for creating something that is completely original, and that reflects your personal tastes. Unlike dinnerware, flatware, and crystal, which are purchased in a store and come in the patterns manufacturers offer, table linens that you make allow you to give your dining table an entirely 'new look' whenever you wish.

Actually, the words 'table linens' are misleading because tablecloths, runners, and napkins may be made of any kind of fabric. And, when it comes to place mats and napkin rings, they can even be made of straw, wood, or plastic, or crocheted or woven of various types of yarn.

Besides the sense of freshness you bring to the dining table with handmade table linens, you can achieve whatever degree of formality pleases you most. The type of entertaining you do and the style of dining that you have for your own family will dictate this choice. Even if you are extremely budget-minded, you can have a variety of table linens if you shop wisely for the material and make them yourself. Don't restrict your shopping to any one area. Browse through dress fabric, drapery fabric, and needlework departments, bedding departments for colorful designer sheets, and import shops where you might find handwoven scarves and natural fiber matting.

You might even find items at home that lend themselves to table linens—an old paisley shawl, a patchwork quilt, or a crocheted bedspread handed down from your grandmother.

You don't have to be an expert seamstress or a whiz at needlecraft to make table linens that are worthy of rave notices. As you explore this chapter, you will find many ideas that you can adapt to your needs regardless of how skilled you are, and regardless of how much time you have to devote to such projects.

← The dining table at the left is covered with a floor-length circular red tablecloth and topped with a bold red, white, and blue plaid square cover. Both are easy to make, using cotton fabric.

Table Linens to Sew

The super-scale graphic print tablecloth pictured above started out as a designer bed sheet. Both the tablecloth and napkins are permanent-press fabrics, thus eliminating time-consuming ironing. You'll find many of the exciting new sheet patterns ideal for the table.

The tablecloth above is made of yard goods in a geometric pattern, reminiscent of American Indian weaving. It provides a dramatic background for jet black plates and white accessories. The small, footed jug holds a loose array of daisies and berried branches.

For those of you who like to have variety in your dining table scenery, there's no more satisfying way to do it than by sewing your own table linens. You can confine your collection to a basic supply of tablecloths, place mats, and table runners, or if you're an avid party-giver, you can indulge in stitching up a large selection of colorful table linens, in both formal styles and the extremely popular casual styles.

Now that there are so many washable, stain-resistant, and permanent-press fabrics, the selection of fabrics for table linens is almost unlimited. The colors, patterns, and textures in both natural and synthetic fibers, and in blends, offer endless possibilities to the creative homemaker who is willing to spend some time and energy making her own table linens.

Tablecloths to Sew

Don't even begin to shop for fabric for a tablecloth unless you are absolutely sure you know the exact size and shape of your dining table. The length and width of your table is very important in selecting a cloth that will look just right. In order to avoid any errors, make a drawing of the tabletop, and add the width and length of the drop to each side and end.

If you wish to make a formal tablecloth, add 16 to 24 inches to both the length and the width of the tabletop. If you plan to make an informal tablecloth, you won't need quite as much drop, usually 10 to 14 inches. Never make a tablecloth with less than 10 inches of fabric to hang over the edges of the table—less looks skimpy.

On the other hand, don't let the tablecloth drag on the floor; the only type of tablecloth that should just barely touch the floor is a banquet cloth.

Never have a seam running down the middle of a tablecloth. If your table is rectangular or square, use one length of fabric down the middle of the table, and join the strips of fabric at either side to achieve whatever width is most suitable.

To make a round tablecloth, first measure the width of the tabletop, then add to this the number of inches of drop to either side. For example, if you have a table with a diameter of 48 inches and you want a 30-inch drop, add 30 inches plus 48 inches plus 30 inches. Use one width of material for the center of the table, and full or split widths of fabric, depending on the width of the fabric, for each side to make a 108-inch square. Stitch the three strips together (if your fabric is patterned, be sure the patterns match), and press the seams open. Spread the fabric out on the floor, and find the center of the cloth. Tie a string to a pencil, and cut the string to 54 inches. Use a thumbtack to hold the end of the string in place, and draw a full circle. Then, cut it out, allowing 1 extra inch for a hem. Stitch the hem by machine or by hand.

The circular tablecloth below, made from a permanent-press sheet, projects a summery mood for an afternoon buffet. The turquoise blue and avocado print is highlighted by turquoise napkins, coordinated candles, salt and pepper shakers, and a space-saving floral centerpiece.

The full-length, red and white striped table-cloth pictured above has a 'parasol' effect that adds another dramatic dimension. It is made of V-shaped bias-cut triangles of cotton yard goods. Save the scraps that are left, and use them to create the pinwheel blooms that spike the bouquet of gladiolus in the slender vase. Alternate pastel yellow octagonal plates with splashy golden geometric patterned ones, and use matching solid color gold napkins.

Fabrics for Tablecloths

One of the best reasons for making your own tablecloths is that there is such a wealth of material from which to choose. There are colors, textures, patterns, and qualities to suit every taste and every budget. For the thrift-minded homemaker, the remnant counter alone will offer a great many opportunities to use creative talents in producing distinctive table covers that are truly original designs.

When you're shopping for fabric, be sure to note the fiber content, as this determines both the price and the wear you can expect. Each bolt should be labeled with laundering instructions and with any other special-care recommendations.

Choose from cottons and cotton blends, handwoven textiles, linens, silks, and rayons. Almost all of the modern-day fabrics have built-in soil release, and are machine washable. The permanent-press finish has banished the traditional chore of ironing from the list of household tasks.

In addition to solid colors in either vivid or subdued tones, you will find candy stripes, lively checks and plaids, realistic florals, and bold geometrics.

Texture, too, enters the picture. There are brocades, applique fabrics, and lace. Even burlap and felt can be made into tablecloths of which you'll be proud.

Just be sure that the fabric you choose is in harmony with the rest of your table-ware—china, crystal, and flatware.

Use the fern drawing above to decorate the tablecloth above at the right. Each square represents one inch. This tablecloth is worthy of a wedding or any formal occasion, and it's easy to make. (Instructions are given on this page.)

Add hurricane lamps and grape clusters that are made from cracked marbles. Such a setting calls for elegant accompaniments such as ornate china, with a heavy gold scroll border, gold banded crystal, and sterling flatware.

To make the fern tablecloth above first cut one panel, plus a seam allowance, to fit the tabletop. Then, cut the side and end panels floor length, and allow for the hems. Cotton organdy was chosen for this tablecloth because its stiffness works well for the machine embroidery.

Embroider the tabletop piece and each of the side panels before joining them. First, draw a fern pattern on a piece of paper (see sketch). Place the pattern under the cloth wherever you want one of the motifs, and trace the pattern on the cloth with a green pencil. Then, consult the manual that comes with your sewing machine for instructions on how to prepare the machine for embroidering. (Feed dogs are lowered on some machines; on others, the plate is raised so the feed dogs do not pull fabric through.) Remove the presser foot. Set stitch length at neutral; loosen the tension slightly before you start to sew.

Use embroidery hoops reversed from the usual way so that the fabric is resting on the machine with edges of hoops standing up at outer edge. Hold the fabric taut by the hoops so the thread will not fray. The faster you move the fabric while sewing, the longer the stitches will be.

After embroidering all of the designs, sew the panels together with flat-fell seams. Turn the edges under, then hem so the sides measure 29 inches (standard).

If you enjoy items that are completely handcrafted, you may choose to hand-embroider these designs instead.

46

Place Mats

Place mats have proved to be such a blessing to today's busy homemakers that it's difficult to imagine how they ever managed without these easy-care table mats.

Place mats range in size from 12 to 14 inches deep and 16 to 18 inches long. The size is important because you may find that eight small place mats will fit on your table comfortably, while a larger size will necessitate cutting down to six place settings.

If you're unsure about what size of place mats to make for your table, draw a paper pattern geared to the tabletop length and width, and make your mats accordingly.

Keep in mind that mats should be large enough to hold a complete place setting without crowding it. And, although place mats do cut down on ironing a great deal,

they also reveal a large portion of the tabletop. So, be sure to keep the tabletop cleaned and polished.

Place mats are so simple to make that there's no excuse for not having a generous supply of them on hand. In many cases, it's simply a matter of hemming rectangles of fabric, and perhaps adding a touch of trim.

At the same time that you are making mats, it's a good idea to make napkins in matching or coordinated colors and fabrics.

When it comes to selecting fabric for place mats, there is no limit. The variety of fabrics ranges all the way from easy-care vinyl-coated ones to elegant embroidered organdies and imported silks. In between these two extremes there are a vast number of cottons, rayons, linens, and blends of two or more fibers in colors and patterns to suit the most discriminating tastes.

The button-diamond-shaped place mats below are made of coordinated fabrics. They may be used individually or as runners teamed with a do-it-yourself centerpiece, which is a floral fantasy made of multicolored buttons. Instructions for place mats are given on page 47.

Denims, striped mattress ticking, drapery fabric, dotted swiss, hand-loomed fabrics, and sailcloth are all likely candidates for place mats, too. Be sure to choose those that have a permanent-press quality, and you'll lighten your ironing load.

It takes very little sewing time—and skill —to whip up a set of place mats and napkins to accompany them. Why don't you try making mats of polka dot fabric edged with rickrack trim, and then make napkins of the same color with very tiny polka dots and edge them with baby rickrack?

Or, for a completely feminine table setting, use pink, blue, or yellow checked gingham, and sew ruffles around the edges. Stitch a band of ribbon on top where the mat joins the ruffle. Make napkins to match, and edge them with the same ribbon.

Make a supply of button-on diamond-shaped place mats, and you'll be prepared for the next time you entertain at a morning brunch or a luncheon. Choose a patterned cotton fabric that harmonizes with your tableware, and team it with two coordinated solid colors—one for the reverse side of the place mats; the other for the napkins.

To make each mat, cut two diamond shapes that measure 19 inches long by 15 inches wide at the points. Place a solid color diamond and a patterned diamond together, right sides together, and stitch a seam around it, leaving a slit long enough so that you can turn it right side out. Overcast this opening shut, and press the place mat well. Make a buttonhole on one end of the widest point, and sew a button on the opposite end. For each napkin, sew a button at one corner and make a buttonhole at the opposite corner of each napkin. When setting the table, button the place mats together, then button the napkins in place.

The matching centerpiece is made of graduated sizes of multicolored buttons. To make these 'posies,' use green florist's wire for the stems. Bend a length of corsage wire through two holes of the smallest buttons. Twist the wire tightly two or three times under the button after threading. Add a slightly larger button and twist again. Continue threading on gradually larger buttons, twisting the wire after each addition.

The fiesta-flavored place mats shown below measure 13¾ inches by 17½ inches. Make them of upholstery webbing, using four strips 3½ inches wide for each one. Join the strips together, using a zigzag stitch on your sewing machine, so that the black edge marks on the webbing are evenly spaced. Fringe the side edges and machine stitch for several rows along the inner edge of the fringe. Use 4-ply knitting worsted yarn in several bright colors to work the embroidery stitches.

Use four rows of running stitches to cover black strip marks. To cover seams where the strips are joined, make large criss-crosses—there are three rows of these.

Between the rows of running stitches, make long straight stitches, as shown, and join them in the middle with a couching stitch. Make six straight stitches in each grouping and make seven groupings across each row, evenly spaced. Add a French knot in the center of each. If you wish, you can back the mats with cotton lining material.

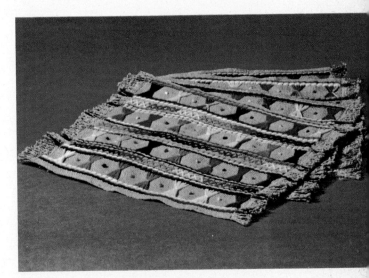

You'll bring fiesta flavor to every meal when you set the table with the peasant-style place mats pictured above. The liveliest colors are used to embroider the mats, and to add to the country airs, the mats are made of rough-textured upholstery webbing strips. You will find complete instructions for these on this page.

The hand-fashioned lace place mats above testify to the fact that it is unnecessary to use fine damask tablecloths in order to set a formal dinner table. Delicately bordered china, graceful stemware, and transitional patterned flatware highlight the romantic effect.

Lace Place Mats

Any imaginative hostess can create the hand-fashioned lace place mats and matching napkins shown in the picture above. First, cut an oval paper pattern that measures 12 inches by 18 inches, and use it to trace around stiff material such as crinoline or organdy for the backing of each place mat.

Next cut a piece of permanent-press cotton or linen in a solid color 1 inch larger than the backing all the way around, place it over the backing, bring the edges underneath, and fasten with iron-on fabric bonding film. Then, cut white lace, which you can buy by the yard in fabric departments, the same size as the solid color fabric, and place it on top of the solid color. Fold edges over to the wrong side, and fasten with iron-on bonding film in the same manner. Cut an oval of felt 11½ inches by 17½ inches, and fasten to the back with fabric adhesive so that all raw edges are concealed. Finish with a coat of soil-resistant spray on the top of the mat. Make napkins of the same solid color that peeks through the lace for a coordinated effect.

If you have some old worn-out place mats of a size and shape that you like, you can cover these in this same manner rather than buying new material for the backing.

Perhaps you would like something less formal for your table. If so, you could use this same technique with a coarse mesh fabric on top of the solid color fabric instead of the delicate lace.

Triangular Place Mats

You can sew the distinctive triangular-shaped place mats and matching napkins shown at the right for your round dining table. These fan-shaped mats are designed for five place settings at a 54-inch-diameter dining table. Cut a triangular paper pattern that is 33 inches by 27 inches with five scallops along the 33-inch side.

Cut out two pieces for each mat if you wish to make them reversible. Then trim each mat with leafy applique motifs toward the center and diamond machine stitching around the entire edge.

Allow a total of five yards of fabric for five reversible place mats. You will have enough fabric left to make triangular-shaped napkins to match the mats.

Vinyl Place Mats

If you have vinyl wall covering in your dining area, why not perk up your dining table with new vinyl place mats that match the wall covering? These are easy to make, even for the inexperienced seamstress.

The petal-shaped vinyl place mats below are of the same vinyl as that on the walls. Instructions for vinyl place mats are on this page.

Triangular-shaped place mats and napkins cover the round table above. Complete directions for making them are given at the left.

To make the petal-shaped vinyl place mats at left, cut the shapes and bind them with black bias tape around the edges. When you are cutting the vinyl material, use masking tape to hold the pattern in place. Snip through the tape as the shape is cut out. (Do not pin through the vinyl, as this will leave permanent holes.) To keep the vinyl from puckering when you are stitching on the bias binding, use a sharp needle.

Grommet the pointed ends of each mat so that you can join the petals with a pronged metal fastener. This will keep the pieces together in the center of the table.

Don't throw away the scraps of vinyl that are left. Cut out single floral motifs and use them to add a festive touch to the napkins that lay folded beside the mats.

Table Runners

One of the best ways to give your tabletop treatment strong eye-appeal is to use table runners. Runners are probably the most recent innovation to appear on tabletops, and they're becoming increasingly popular because of their flexibility.

You can make runners in the same wide variety of fabrics and synthetics that you would use for either tablecloths or place mats. There is also fabric specially woven for table runners. All you have to do is buy the length you need, and hem or fringe the ends. There are many colors and designs in this runner fabric, and there are even many that are handloomed.

Runners should be approximately 12 inches deep, and they may either fit the length of your table exactly or have a drop on both ends of from 8 to 10 inches. They may be made of a single length of material hemmed around the edges, or they may be a double thickness of fabric, in which case they can be reversible. In addition, the ends may be scalloped or come to a point.

Usually, runners are used on either side of the table and may hold numerous place settings. However, for additional place settings, you can use a center runner, which holds the two place settings at each end of the table, and arrange harmonizing place mats along the sides of the table.

The brown and beige table runner and place mats below are reversible. One side features broad stripes, and the other side has diminutive checks. The table runner is trimmed with two buckles that match the design of the china on the striped side. For an interesting variation, alternate the checks and stripes as shown in the picture, or use them all alike.

Sturdy cotton fabric is well suited for this type of runner. For both runner and mats, place two pieces of fabric right sides together and stitch around them, leaving an opening long enough to turn them to the right side. Overcast the opening by hand,

Here's an interesting way to combine a table runner, place mats, and two patterns of dinnerware and flatware. The centerpiece is a mod pottery container holding an arrangement of marigolds, pods, and quaint cottage blooms made from folded bias strips of checked fabric.

Runners that cross in the center of the table are especially attractive on a round or square table. Directions for these are given below.

Supergraphic designs in vivid colors on the table runners above and the centerpiece of fruit highlight a simply designed dining table.

and press them. Then, attach the brown trim and the buckles to the runner. You can vary the color according to the color of your china and glassware.

The tie-dye runners above are made from 32x74-inch strips of white cotton fabric. To make them, wash the fabric first, and while the fabric is still damp, lay it out flat. Fold it in half lengthwise. Starting at one end, fold the corner over even to the edge so that it forms a triangle. Continue folding under and over until all the fabric is triangular in shape. Tie rubber bands around each corner.

Mix ½ cup of liquid dye into two quarts of hot water. Heat it to simmering. Add the damp tied fabric, and stir it often for 20 minutes. Remove the fabric, and rinse it in warm water. Remove the rubber bands, and rinse the fabric until the water is clear. Add one tablespoonful of liquid detergent,

then wash and rinse the material. Dry the fabric in the dryer, then press it. Finally, cut the fabric in half lengthwise, and hem all of the edges.

The brightly colored table runners above are ideal for those who have contemporary furnishings and tableware.

For the side runners, select a fabric with a gigantic pattern in bold colors that are harmonious with your furnishings and your tableware. Choose a matching solid color for the end runners.

Measure the length of your dining table, and make the side runners long enough so that there is an 8- or 10-inch drop at either end. Also, make the solid color end runners wide enough so that they can drop an equal amount from the table edge. This will give a unified appearance to both ends of the table. Make napkins of another color that appears in the print design.

Table Covers to Paint

This peony and butterfly runner is perfect for a luncheon. Notice that the design is painted with short strokes to simulate stitches.

For this variation of the paint-and-linen technique, cut out a pattern adapted from the plate design, and paint it on mats and napkins.

If you're the type of person who enjoys wielding a paintbrush rather than painstakingly stitching embroidery designs, you will enjoy making table covers like those shown on these two pages.

For the linens shown above, use ready-made mats, runners, and cloths (stamped for embroidery) and fabric paints that come with their own easy-to-use dispensers. Most needlework departments have linens similar to these, and the variety shops carry textile paints in many colors.

You can make these linens quickly and easily. Paint the printed outlines with as many colors as you wish—fill in the solid areas as indicated; add the fine shadings last. When dry, press with a hot iron to set the colors. You can launder these distinctive table covers many times without any possibility of fading.

The hardboard place mats shown on the next page do require some time and patience, but they are well worth the effort.

You can find most of the supplies at your building supply dealer. Get ¼-inch hardboard and cut the mats 10x14 inches. (For a small charge your supplier will cut them for you.) Buy enamel for the background of the mats and marine varnish for the finishing coats. Purchase a small can of gold paint (not spray paint) and some all-purpose adhesive. You will need ¼-inch, 1-inch, and 2-inch flat-edged paintbrushes. Also, purchase some 1/16-inch-wide gold adhesive-backed tape.

You can find pictures for mounting on the mats at museum shops, craft supply stores, art shops, even antique or thrift shops. You may even have some tucked away that you have been saving.

Choose your pictures carefully, and the end product should be an art object worthy of decorating a wall, as well as being used as a place mat. When selecting the pictures, follow these few rules:

1. Select pictures of the same size.

2. Make sure there is continuity of subject matter in the pictures.

3. The thickness of most art prints works well. A thinner picture may not withstand the glue beneath and the lacquer above. A thicker picture would not permit a relatively smooth finished product.

4. Select pictures that have a matte finish rather than a glossy one. This allows the varnish to adhere securely. Sealing the mats is very important because you will wipe them often with a damp cloth.

Here are the step-by-step directions for making these handsome place mats:

1. Sand the edges of each piece of hardboard with medium sandpaper, then sand the corners to round them slightly.

2. Cut pieces of cardboard slightly smaller than the picture size. Place them in the center of the hardboard pieces, and paint uncovered area with two coats of enamel. Use a 1-inch paintbrush.

3. Paint the edges with two coats of gold, using the ¼-inch paintbrush.

4. Glue the pictures in the center.

5. Apply the gold tape all around each picture, ⅛ inch from the pictures.

6. Use marine varnish over the surface and edges—a minimum of three coats is necessary. Sand between coats with extra-fine sandpaper or steel wool.

7. Cut adhesive-backed felt into 9½x13½-inch pieces, center them on the bottom of the mats, and attach them. This will prevent mats from scratching your table.

These place mats can be wiped clean after each meal, and they can even be used as wall hangings between meals. Use them as individual place mats only, never as mats to hold hot serving dishes.

The place mats below truly are works of art. They are made of hardboard with art prints mounted on top. Complete instructions for making them are given on these pages. Notice how they also can be used as attractive wall hangings when not being used on the table.

Quick-and-Easy Table Covers

Every so often an occasion comes along when you want to add sparkle to your dining table by covering it with something new and different. Very often, when you feel this urge, there isn't time to make something that requires many hours of handwork. That's why the table covers in this section are so useful—each can be made quickly.

However, before you rush out to buy some exotic or simple fabric or some elegant cushiony felt or other material, take a close look at all the remnants you have tucked away in closets and drawers around the home. You'll be pleasantly surprised to see how effective a handmade patchwork quilt, a cherished crocheted bedspread, or a similar family heirloom looks when it is placed on the table and used as a table cover.

Felt Table Covers

Highly appropriate for special-occasion entertaining and holidays, felt really fits into the quick-and-easy category. It is inexpensive, comes in widths up to 72 inches, is available in many colors, and is always most easy to work with.

It can be used equally well for tablecloths, place mats, and runners. Because felt is nonwoven, it does not ravel and needs no hemming or finishing of edges unless you wish to edge it with braid or fringe. You can cut it with either a regular or pinking shears, and you can add your own decorative trim. Remember that felt is not washable, so it's a good idea to apply a coat of soil-resistant spray.

Everyone loves a 'cutup,' and that's all it takes to make the white felt tablecloth shown at the bottom of this page.

Make a pattern and trace it on the wrong side of the tablecloth, moving the pattern as necessary until all the felt has been covered with motifs. Cut out the designs and place the felt over a silver vinyl undercover to establish a sparkling theme.

To create the unusual tablecloth below, all you need is a piece of felt and a pair of scissors. Made of white felt, it is placed over a silver *vinyl undercloth and teamed with sterling flatware, white plates, and clear crystal stemware. Use drawing as a guide.*

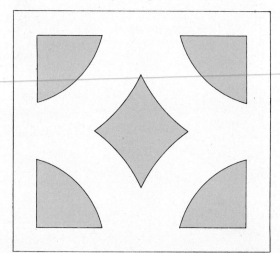

The red, black, and white color scheme of this setting starts with a patterned paper runner used over a red linen tablecloth. Add easy-care paper plates and cups, and for contrast, silver goblets, and silver container with dried foliage and red poppies arranged around it.

Paper Table Covers

You can achieve elegance with ease by using paper products to cover the table.

Gift wrap paper is available in so many beautiful colors and designs that it offers many possibilities for table covers, mats, and runners. Even some of the shelf papers are worthy of topping a dining table.

Designer Sheets for Tabletops

You can have an entire wardrobe of table covers at little expense if you use colorful, patterned, permanent-press bed sheets. You won't even have to worry about seams when using sheets because you can choose all the way from twin- to king-size sheets. These are great for circular table covers, too. Use them also to make napkins.

Burlap Table Covers

Don't overlook good, old-fashioned burlap when you're groping for ideas for quick-and-easy table linens. New versions of this old standby are washable, have a permanent-press finish, come in several widths, and are available in a color range that includes both vivid and subdued hues.

You can use burlap to make tablecloths, place mats, or runners. If you are making a tablecloth, be sure to measure your table carefully and follow the instructions given on page 42. If your material has to be pieced, let a full panel run down the center with piecing at either side—never have a seam down the middle of the table.

You can hem burlap table covers, fringe them, or finish them with an edging of braid or other trim. Remember that burlap frays easily, so make an allowance for this when you are measuring and cutting. Make the hem wide enough so that threads will not pop out. If you plan to fringe the edges, make one row of machine stitching at the edge of the fringe so that it will not ravel beyond the stitched line.

You can embroider on burlap, applique motifs on it, or paint designs on it, as well as using a solid color alone. Go one step further and make napkins of sturdy cotton fabric, and decorate them to harmonize with the cloth, runners, or mats.

The rough texture of burlap is especially compatible with handcrafted ceramic tableware in earth tones, or contemporary tableware in either bold or neutral hues.

Try Your Hand at Trays

Who would ever think you could fashion festive serving trays from all sorts of unlikely articles such as clipboards, inexpensive picture frames, and even lids from boxes? These trays can simplify serving, and at the same time, double as place mats. Even though they are so simple to make that you can enlist your children to lend a hand, they can still give a catered look to spur-of-the-moment entertaining.

The stocking box lid at the right is ideal for tots' parties. It is just the right size to hold a bowl that can be used for both ice cream and cake or cookies, and a mug for juice or milk. Just line the lid with gaily striped gift wrap or adhesive-backed paper, and outline the edge with silver tape to add a finishing touch.

A standard 11x14-inch picture frame, which you can buy inexpensively at a variety or discount store, can also serve as a place mat-tray. If you are in doubt about

The natural-colored burlap tablecloth below is simple to make, even for the all-thumbs seamstress. It is centered with an arrangement of *oak leaves and dried flowers, and old French sterling flatware is combined with china and wine goblets of contemporary design.*

your artistic ability, design your own version of pop art simply by cutting letters from magazines or posters and combining them with pieces of burlap.

Or, for a change of pace, use fabric with bold designs and colors under the glass, and make napkins of the same fabric.

Slip the finished art underneath the glass, replace the backing, and tape it shut. For maximum visual impact, use glass plates on the picture frame place mats.

Clipboard trays are just right for a combination business meeting and lunch. When the luncheon is over, present each of the guests with one of the novel trays.

To make these unusual trays, first paint the entire surface of the clipboard with poster paint. When the paint is completely dry, give the clipboard a coat of clear lacquer to add durability. Cut ¼-inch dowels to fit three sides, and glue them in place with white glue ½ inch from the edge. This rim prevents the plates from slipping off. The clip holds the napkin.

Stocking box lids, lined with gift wrap paper, are surprisingly sturdy. These box lid trays are made to order for children's parties.

It's a 'frame-up' for your table when you use picture frames that do double duty as place mats and hand serving trays.

Clipboard trays, each with a paper napkin fastened in the clip, make snacks maneuverable and can be presented to guests as favors.

Place Mats to Build

It's not often that you find place mats for the handyman to build, but the fish place mats below are a good example of what you can create with a little lumber, tubing, a hammer, and a saw.

The mats are made of 1-inch pine lumber. For each one you'll need two 1x4x12-inch pieces and seven 1x1x14-inch pieces, 36 inches of ¼-inch aluminum tubing, and 8 inches of ⅜-inch plastic tubing (center opening should be ¼ inch) cut into ½ inch pieces. You'll also need contact cement, sandpaper, and stain or finish.

To make the place mats, cut and sand the head and tail pieces, using the sketch below as a guide. Then, mark and drill holes for tubing through the head and part way

through the tail, as shown in the sketch. Drill the eye hole in the fish head. (Place it so it doesn't interfere with holes for the tubing.) Mark and drill holes in slats used for body of fish. Sand, then stain or finish all wood parts before assembling them.

To assemble, mark the middle of the piece of aluminum tubing and bend it gently at this point. Bend it around a glass or can until it is shaped like a big hairpin. Slide the tubing through the head, then slip on two ½-inch pieces of plastic tubing to act as spacers for the body slats. (Tubing will be easier to put on aluminum if you drop the sections into hot water.

Continue alternating slats and plastic spacers over aluminum tubing. At the tail, check length of the aluminum tubes for fit. Cut them off with a hacksaw if they're too long. Put contact glue into holes of tail piece and on ends of tubing, and push tubing into tail. Allow it to dry.

Mark outline of fish on body slats and saw them off. Finish ends of pieces.

Here's a real catch—fish place mats that can hang on the wall for storage and decoration when they are not in service at mealtime.

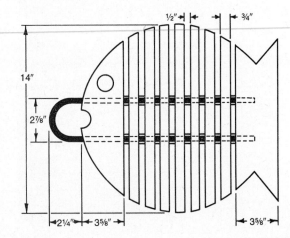

Use the sketch below as a guide for cutting out head and tail pieces. After sanding and staining, add a polyurethane finish if you want extra protection for your fish place mats.

Customizing Ready-Mades

When time is at a premium and you're eager to inject a new and lively note into your table settings, create something completely original by adding your own decoration to ready-made table linens. Either buy inexpensive tablecloths, place mats, table runners, and napkins or look through your linen closet for table linens that will lend themselves to a decorative treatment. Then, apply the trim of your choice.

When you are deciding what treatment to give your table linens, keep in mind the color and design of your tableware. You can repeat a design that appears on your dinnerware by appliquing motifs of fabric on your linens. It could be a large, dominant design or simply a border design.

In the photo below, only place mats are shown, but these same treatments can be used on other table linens as well—tablecloths, runners, and napkins.

The yellow place mat is made of a double layer of organdy with a wide satin border. The butterflies were cut from chintz and appliqued on by hand.

The black place mat is decorated with a rather large and bold motif cut from a scrap of drapery fabric and applied to the mat with a permanent fabric bonding film.

The orange straw mat features embroidery stitches done with knitting worsted.

The blue linen place mat is banded at either side with a 3-inch-wide strip of a patchwork quilt stitched in place.

The grouping of place mats shown below is only a small sampling of various techniques that can be adapted to customizing ready-made table linens. By using your ingenuity, you can expand this list to include many more ways to decorate cloths, mats, runners, and napkins.

Making Napkins and Napkin Rings

For the past few years there has been a marked revival of interest in cloth napkins. Most likely, this is due to the fact that there is such a wide variety of fabrics in all colors and designs that are easy to launder and require little or no ironing.

There was a time when many napkins remained in a linen drawer most of the time because they weren't suitable—either they were too tiny to be practical or they required special care that made washing and ironing a tedious chore.

Now, most cottons and even the finest linens have a permanent-press finish. As a result, napkins have regained the popularity and wide usage that they once had.

Along with this trend, it's only natural that napkin rings should share the limelight with napkins. The number of designs and shapes you can make and the materials you can use are almost endless.

Making Napkins

The most important feature to consider when making napkins is the size. Dinner napkins may be 18, 20, 22, or 24 inches square; luncheon and breakfast napkins 17 inches square; tea napkins 12 inches square; and cocktail napkins 4x6 or 6x8 inches. For buffet dinners, 12x18-inch rectangular napkins are a good choice—a favorite with men because they can spread it across their knees without it falling off.

Hemming napkins by hand is a must for dinner napkins, but for the other sizes neat machine stitching is acceptable.

Making Napkin Rings

The napkin rings that are shown at the bottom of these two pages are just a few examples of types that you can make.

The napkin rings below point out so well what these small accessories can do to add special interest to your table settings. They are easy to make, require very little space for storage, and can be whisked out at mealtime for use with harmonizing table linens and tableware.

The napkin ring at the left (opposite page) is made of three pipe cleaners (each one a different color) braided and shaped around a piece of mailing tube. Twist ends of the braid around each other to join them, and curl the ends around a pencil to create a spiral effect. You can make these in a few minutes, and at little cost.

The center napkin ring (opposite page) has a wooden drapery ring for a base. Crochet around the ring with yarn so that it is completely covered, and attach several small yarn pompons in contrasting colors.

The napkin ring at the right (opposite page) can be as simple or as ornate as you desire. You'll need to purchase some 2-inch brass plumbing pipe at a plumbing supply shop. To make the napkin ring, first cut the pipe in 1½-inch widths. Then, incise the design of your choice on it with a woodworking tool. If you want the design more sharply etched, heat the tool so it will penetrate the metal further.

Needlepoint napkin rings like the ones below can be worked in any combination of colors that complement your tableware.

The napkin rings that are shown below feature an unusual design consisting of a circle of tulips stitched on a long strip of canvas. Use a section of a cardboard mailing tube as a core.

For each napkin ring, work the design that is shown on the diagrams below on a 7x4-inch strip of 10-mesh-to-the-inch needlepoint canvas. When you have completed the stitchery, trim the canvas, leaving ½ inch of canvas around the edges. Crease along all the edges of the work, and press the edges underneath.

With a sewing needle, weave the ends of the strip together. Insert a cardboard core, 1⅝ inches in diameter, within the canvas strip. For a core, slice a 1½-inch piece of a mailing tube with a sharp knife. Turn the edges of the canvas to the inside of the core, clipping if necessary to avoid bulk. For lining, cut a 5-inch piece of grosgrain ribbon that is 1½ inches wide. At one end, turn under one inch and press. Insert the ribbon inside the core with the pressed edge on top of the raw edge. Whipstitch the needlepoint to the ribbon lining.

Follow the diagrams below to make the napkin rings at the right. Use 10-mesh canvas and a blunt tapestry needle and wool yarn.

Begin at upper left-hand corner of canvas, and work stitches in half cross-stitch from left to right, keeping stitches in same direction.

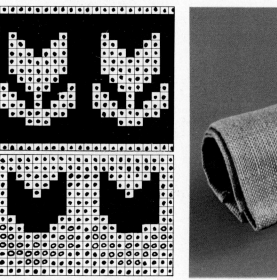

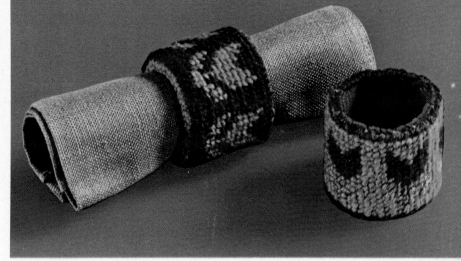

Centerpieces and Table Decorations

Memorable tables start with exciting centerpieces or table decorations. They are the finishing touches that are essential to the overall harmony of a table. A centerpiece makes a large table with many place settings seem warm and inviting. Decorations also unify and soften a sea of serving pieces on a buffet table.

These tabletop highlights are as varied as the people who use them. Flowers and greenery are favorites of many. Use blossoms from the garden as well as from the florist. Or, for a simple, effective, and inexpensive decoration select three large hot house blooms and surround them with foliage. Dried flowers will last through many meals. And spark up a bowl of fruit that becomes a centerpiece and dessert in one by adding shiny green leaves or daisies.

← *You can make the morning meal more memorable with an easy decoration. A humble ice cream glass holding a handful of daisies will add a touch of personal magic. Simple decorations are often quite dramatic.*

Go on a treasure hunt in your own home, and discover hidden sources for decorations. Be inventive with containers. Consider odd bits of crockery from long-forgotten sets, or use clusters of putty-colored marmalade jars. Spruce up ordinary jugs or plastic bottles with spray paint for original and unique containers.

Found objects, so long as they are attractive, can be used as the focus of interest on a table. Try shells, small sculptures, paper fans, paperweight collections — anything you love yourself. Use them with greenery and flowers, or let them stand alone in their own special glory.

For special occasions, select decorations that convey the feeling you're trying for. Some holidays, when informal, call for all-out efforts.

More restrained decorations suit some occasions best, as for a formal afternoon tea. Here, a traditional floral centerpiece in pastels would give an elegant air. Keep your everyday decorations fresh and exciting, and mealtime will become so, too. Surprise the family with special tables for important personal events.

Choosing Centerpieces and Decorations

To set a truly interesting table, you need to provide a focal point. Many elements can be used as accessories to the place settings, including candles, bon-bon dishes, individual decorated place cards, and fancy napkin folds. But to pull it all together, have one major piece. Think of your centerpiece as the dominant piece on which the eye immediately focuses.

Suit the centerpiece to the table appointments. Have it echo the lines of your flatware and glassware, or pick up the colors of your china. A centerpiece coordinated with table linen colors gives an immediate unifying effect. Match the flowers in a damask design or on china with real-life renditions in a colorful bouquet.

For beginners, it is easiest to arrange all the necessary elements on the table and then to decide on the dimensions and style of the centerpiece. Make sure that it does not crowd any of the place settings or the serving dishes. For the best effect, make table decorations a different height than glassware. The decorations will then give added depth and dimension to the table, making it come alive.

For sit-down meals, experiment with the placement of centerpieces in locations other than the center. Place two matching arrangements on a long, narrow table, or place table arrangements at the end of the table. This is especially good when the table adjoins a wall. Try many formats.

Fern leaves are used for an off-center arrangement when settings are on one side of the table. This high arrangement will not impede any diner's view. The shape of the leaves is echoed in the design of the center of the bowl.

Tea roses coupled with rich green leaves are displayed in a high container. Each flower head is given ample room to open. A ceramic bird placed below returns the eye to the flowers. Long, diagonally placed leaves add width.

The flower shapes reoccur continually in this white and yellow arrangement. With strongly patterned cloths or mats such as these, keep *the flowers simple and monochromatic. Notice how the use of real daisies ties the table together. The candle is well above eye level.*

Flowers are naturals for tables, and have been for over 2,000 years. In Roman times, certain flowers were considered good antidotes to overindulgence, so they were set on the table. Today, flowers are chosen for their magic powers of enchantment.

Always place formal flower arrangements in the table's center. Make sure they look good from all directions. And check that they do not overwhelm the setting or the diners. The easiest overall dimension to achieve in creating formal arrangements is a cone shape or globe shape. Here, mass-produced flowers of uniform size are best.

Consider making permanent formal arrangements from silk, china, or dried flowers. Even plastic ones, artfully chosen, can be elegant. Such arrangements will be beauti-

ful between meals, too, since they can be left right on the table. Elegant silver or crystal containers suit the formal flower arrangements best.

Informal floral arrangements take as much organizing as do the formal ones, but they have a casual look when finished. Use strong textures and colors in any flowers that are available at the time. Mix them together for an exuberant result.

Make sure containers and contents are in keeping with each other. For example, match flower colors to the container tone. Rustic pottery, brass or tinware, or lined baskets are good holders for casual arrangements. Trial and error will lead you to the best flowers for each container, so be as adventurous as you wish.

Add the Charm of Candles

Whether they are round, tall, square, chunky, or pristinely tapered, candles add character and charm to a table. For formal dinners, they are essential. Use only the sleek, tapered kind of any diameter, and make sure they are tall enough to be above eye level when guests are seated.

Formal white candles, in the past, meant odorless wax instead of smelly, smudging tallow. Today, traditionalists prefer pure white, while modernists use colored tapers.

Pick whites or pastels to reflect in the surface of a bare table. Dark-colored candles seem to give off less light than do lighter colored ones, so use more of them. One per diner is the minimum; use more to be sure the food can be seen easily. Light them only after twilight, and see your table setting dramatically come to life.

Anchoring candles securely is easy, once you know some tricks. Use a pellet of florist's clay in the holder, after trimming the candle base if necessary. Or run hot water over the base for a few minutes, then press it into the holder. And make certain that the holder itself is stable and untippable. Be absolutely sure that the candle flame cannot touch anything flammable . . . either when the candle is first lit or when it has burned down quite a lot.

Informal candles can be so striking that they can stand alone as a centerpiece. Accent them with inventive holders. For example, use upended goblets for round or fat candles; group fat candles of different heights and colors on a plate.

You can make any container an attractive candleholder by surrounding the base with greenery or flowers, or a circlet of unshelled nuts or pine cones in the winter.

Pristine white candleholders are perfectly beautiful with sleek, traditional tapers. They are arranged in triangle, with a crystal duck figurine adding grace and movement to the setting. His gaze pulls yours back to the candles.

Stately tapers in different colors placed in square prism holders give a hedgerow effect when they are clustered together. Candles offer wonderful ways of decorating with pure line, plus variety in color.

Ideas Right Before Your Eyes

Many exciting centerpieces result from looking around a home for objects that are packed away and out of sight. For example, simply arranging some greenery around a piece of sculpture transforms it into an arresting and attractive focal point.

Consider using greenery or flowers around a sculptured piece to create a miniature garden. Adding greenery softens the starkness of single pieces and helps to fit them into the best shape for the table. Also, you can unify a collection of figurines by using some greenery.

Scale greenery to the size of the object you plan to use. Use small-leafed greenery for groupings of small objects; consider large, exotic greenery for one starkly contemporary piece. Delicate objects look best with formal or airy leaves and flowers.

Don't overlook your groceries for ideas for exciting and edible centerpieces. Take advantage of the variety of textures, colors, and shapes in fruits for succulent centerpieces. Pyramids of matched fruits are effective, especially when color-coordinated to your dining room decor or table setting. Pick a pretty container and fill it with handpicked red or golden apples. Grapes accessorize well with almost any fruit, and they drape gracefully.

Vegetables make vibrant centerpieces, too. Use them for informal tables, especially in the kitchen. Try rich red onions and peppers with green broccoli or cabbages for an unusual Christmas centerpiece. You can even combine fruits and vegetables.

Keep centerpieces sprightly by removing any tired elements each day. Sometimes, the main arrangement can stay as it is. If it can't, fill in with new additions.

This bowl of fruit centerpiece will brighten any breakfast table. Rich green leaves accent the rounded shapes of the fruit. This decoration takes only creativity, for the fruit is eaten. Remove and use any tired edibles.

These are just a few examples of kitchen tools and gadgets that lend themselves to centerpieces and table decorations. Combine two or more of them, and you can create a decoration that will add interest to your tabletop.

How to Buy Centerpieces and Table Decorations

It is doubtful that you'll be satisfied with a centerpiece if you use a container you do not like. So, build up a collection of vases and figurines or other objects that you want to work with. Favorite pieces will be used time and again, so choose wisely.

Pick containers that enhance the other elements on the table. Have the largest variety of centerpiece props for the set of dinnerware you use most often. If you have few formal dinners per year and almost always use florist flowers, consider investing in only a few smashing vases for such occasional use. If you invariably use the same variety and color of party flowers, get containers that suit them best.

Work with the florist from whom you order centerpiece floral arrangements. He will give you advice and guidance and tell you which flowers are the best buys during that time of year. Drop off your vase at the florist shop at least one day in advance of a party if you wish to use your own container. It's also a good idea to tell him the overall dimensions of your table.

Always ask for a few additional flowers for last-minute changes you might want to make once the flowers are in place. If the arrangement does not need them, use these additional individual flowers at each place setting. Or, use them to make a mini-bouquet for sideboard or powder room.

Pick centerpiece accessories that will amuse your friends and reflect your own interests. A humorous ceramic sculpture of a woman golfer makes a hole-in-one for a spring luncheon table. Sprigs of flowers soften the starkness of using figurines by themselves.

Florists usually have a number of simple containers on hand that are relatively inexpensive. But don't forget that you can have a lot of fun collecting containers. Scour curio shops and antique stores for offbeat containers. You can restore even whimsical pieces to glory with polish and care, making them one-of-a-kind centerpieces that spark table conversation.

Variety shops and supermarkets are good hunting grounds for centerpiece holders, too. Look for inexpensive copies of crocks and Early American glassware to dress with flowers. Or, fill ordinary produce baskets with dried arrangements.

Even cookware departments can yield unusual and charming finds. Try a grouping of deep baking dishes or brioche tins. Or use bottles to hold candles, dried flowers, or fresh flowers. Also consider what spray-painting would do to many objects that might be lurking in the cupboards, attic, or basement of your own home.

Most hollow ware serving pieces lend themselves to flower arrangements. The classic Paul Revere bowl, for example, is an elegant holder for flowers or fruit.

Not all exciting centerpiece ideas begin at home or at the florist shop. Take advantage of trips by looking for usuable momentos to display on your table. Handcrafted local pottery is a good buy in most parts of the United States. Unusual pieces from abroad will give pleasure at home and serve as reminders of a wonderful adventure.

Most countries are noted for a particular kind of ware: tinware in Mexico, Blue Delft in Holland, Country faience in France, or pewter in England. You'll save money by buying things where they are designed and made. It is like bringing part of the country right into your own dining area.

One easy way to match centerpiece containers to other table appointments is to choose things from the same period. Here, two old washstand pitchers are filled with flowers and greenery. With tall containers, leave the flowers short.

You don't have to have a candle in every candleholder. Here, one candle and one carefully chosen branch of green leaves are placed in the low ceramic candleholders to achieve a starkly simple, contemporary table decoration.

Making Centerpieces and Decorations

Making your own centerpieces provides a personal satisfaction that no trip to the florist can match. The results are uniquely your own. The doing gives you a chance to let your creativity have its full reign.

Changing your table arrangements often can be, creatively, as interesting as changing entire room schemes...but without the hassle or headaches of anything so major and so expensive. In fact, the table is a perfect place for trying out new color schemes you are considering for major redecorating. Flowers and greenery, including the dried variety, are available in every color. If a combination you are considering palls at the table, try another.

On the other hand, use daring combinations that you would like to try, but not to live with, joyfully at the table. For instance, hot Mexican combinations of pink, red, and orange are exciting in table-size doses but perhaps too much by the roomful.

Be adventurous. Often, the most smashing combinations are achieved through chance. Since you are working with relatively small elements, be fearless in arranging and rearranging until you have achieved the best effect. Give each container consideration before selecting the one you think is best. If the contents fight the one you select, think nothing of changing in midstream.

Often, flowers or greenery will dictate the containers best for them. As you make different centerpieces, remember the easy combinations and use them as a mainstay.

Crafting your own centerpieces will save you both time and money. Centerpieces that can be saved and reused pay for themselves in the long run. You do it with Christmas decorations, why not with other accent pieces? Even imperfections are on your side with crafted centerpieces, for they show the individual creativity that went into them.

Craft papers of all kinds are ideal materials for table decorations, so long as you never use the decorations near candle flames. Try origami fold figures and shapes.

You might even want to get the youngsters to help. Display them either on the table or suspended from stripped twigs.

Once you have mastered making paper flowers, try a variety of shapes and sizes. To make flowers like those shown below, cut about six inches of crepe paper across a whole package for petals. Cut another two-inch strip for the center.

For the stem, use florist's wire. Gather and flute the smaller paper, and hook it through an end of the wire bent down. Unfold the petal paper, and shape petals by fluting the edges and by stretching the center of each petal. Wrap the bottom petal paper edge around the wire, gathering it as you turn. Finish it with masking tape beneath. Make as many as you need.

Paper flowers are carefully separated from the candles in this make-believe Mexican table setting. Funnels are attached at each end with silver-sprayed cardboard cores. The trim is pocket mirrors outlined in fringed colored foil.

This long, layered candle is designed to exactly suit the long table. Six wicks work as one. To make the candle, pour layers of col-ored wax into a planter. Tumblers holding assortments of flowers in the same color as those in the candle are at either end of the table.

Be crafty with candles, too, for they are the footlights to the staging of a table. The light from candles is flattering to both men and women, regardless of age. Because it is, use it to create the atmosphere that will make most people feel at home, and attractively at their best.

Character candles of every possible size, shape, and shade are available. Some are works of art, and are priced accordingly. Others are less expensive. Both gift and variety stores are good sources for the equipment needed to make your own candles. If you are new to candlemaking, you might consider using a do-it-yourself kit.

Candlemaking is easy, but not for children too young, because it involves using hot wax. Collect interesting shapes in disposable used containers, and make a whole batch of candles at once. Use milk and cream containers, plastic detergent holders, or specially designed forms, plus anything else that comes to mind.

Scenting your own candles is great fun, but keep in mind that the scent should be compatible with the flowers you're using with them. Sandalwood scented candles, for example, would fight ferociously with lilac blooms; heavy, overpowering scents of any kind can interfere with the enjoyment of a meal. Advance planning avoids this.

And don't overlook the possibility of recycling your old candles. It's relatively easy to transform stubs of various colored candles into new layered candles. If your friends have not already caught onto this idea, ask them for all of their used candle ends. Then, you can surprise them by returning the discards as brand-new, beautiful candle creations.

If you find someone else who shares your enthusiasm for candlemaking, suggest working together. Pooling your resources in colors results in almost unlimited possibilities. Husbands often get intrigued by this simple art form, too.

Watching small plants grow in this miniature greenhouse will enthrall youngsters while they eat their breakfast. The place mat, napkin ring, and candleholders are easy to make from folded 3-inch squares of colored tissue paper.

Houseplants Are Perfect

Houseplants are always attractive additions to a table. As such, they are an important element to consider. Use floor-standing varieties to offset a dining area that is open to the rest of the home. Or, create an almost tropical feeling in a small dining space with an elegant arrangement of greenery. Medium-high plants are handsome on buffet tables, centered or to the side or end of the table.

Use your favorite plants alone or in combinations. A full plant, particularly one in bloom, may be decoration enough for a single centerpiece. Some plants just naturally grow to good centerpiece shape and

size. Others will need supplementing. With dark plants be sure to use sufficient lighting so that the leaves and patterns can be seen easily by everyone.

A good pot for growing is rarely a beauty to behold. So, be inventive in hiding the pot. Cover it with foil, then crepe paper or even fabric. Nestle pots in foil-lined wooden bowls or baskets. Foil alone may be enough, if you put pots into silver or pewter containers. Disguise soil with moss from the florist, white pebbles, or gravel. It is the greenery you want to see, not the cultivator's handiwork.

Combine potted plants with flowers for highly unusual and lush arrangements. Houseplants often resemble the leaves of flowers, making such combinations look natural. When working with plants, use a variety of flowers, but avoid those with lots of leaves or hairy stems.

Consider buying plants for just this purpose, for with the addition of only a few flowers, a beautiful arrangement is yours. Start with a block of Oasis or Florapak from a florist. Cut out holes the size of the pots, and slide the pots in. Angle them so that the plants overflow the container gracefully.

Next, decide where to place the flowers. Thick-stemmed flowers can be put into prewatered Oasis. For most fragile flowers, use special individual holders. Try pill bottles, cigar tubes, or individual bud vases. If nothing around the house is suitable, you can buy special cones from a florist. Creeper blossoms will last with a water-filled party balloon tied to the stem.

These arrangements are real cost-cutters. They fill overly large containers at a fraction of the cost of fresh-cut flowers. Change the few flowers used in them, either by variety or color, to create a fresh, new look. Water the plants as usual, and be sure to groom them frequently.

If your thumb tends toward black more than green, consider a terrarium—a miniature landscape created in a see-through enclosed container, where the plants produce their own proper environment. They need virtually no care. Collect mosses, rocks, and mini-tree seedlings during a woodland walk, or invest in an expert arrangement from a florist. These are good choices where plant growing is difficult.

Long Life Starts in the Picking

The secret of long-lasting flower arrangements is to choose cut flowers before they reach their prime. There is nothing more disappointing than having blooms droop.

Cut bulb flowers while they are in the bud stage. Buy florist's flowers while they are in bud, if possible. Follow these guidelines, and your flowers will last longer.

Also check the stamens of flowers. Clip yellow stamen tips before arranging to avoid permanent staining. This either indicates that the flower has already reached or even passed into maturity. The first stages of wilting have begun. Choosing fresher flowers will add days of life to all your floral arrangements.

Some flowers, such as chrysanthemums, do not have the stamens revealed. So, check these double or full-petaled flowers for little threadlike anthers rising above the petals. The centers will be tight enough to make a little dimple if still fresh. Pass over any cut flowers with telltale slime, decomposing foliage, or brown stains on their life-giving stems.

Morning is the best time for cutting your own blooms for two reasons: After a cool night, they have had ample moisture; and you will beat the bees that want to pollinate them and speed maturation. It is easiest to catch buds in the morning.

Pick daisies when the outside petals are open, but the little blooms in the center are still tight. Gather gladiolus and other flowers that blossom in the same way when color is just in the lowest floret. Remove tired bottom blooms and enjoy upper blooms that will open later on in the house.

Roses are indeed unique, even in their best picking time. They are said to last longest in sunny weather if they are cut at midday. If picked too young, they will not open properly. Check that the points of the green crown beneath the bud are bent downward. At lease one petal should be growing away from the mass. If you have picked a bud too early, split that green protective calyx of sepals away so that it does not constrict the opening flower.

Moisture loss is a flower's worst enemy. Transport blooms in well-sealed non-absorbent paper or plastic bag, leaves still on. Allow enough room for an air pocket above their heads. Do not water them first.

Once you're home, give the flowers a good, deep drink below the water line in non-shocking tepid water. Leave the leaves on, as a flower uses them for drinking, too. Air bubbles in the stems can halt the whole drinking process, so re-cut the stems under water. Cut french-bean slant style to allow ample surface for absorption. For woody stems, crush or split ¼ inch upwards. Remove excess leaves below water.

Red and white flowers arranged in pint berry box containers provide the focal point for this country-style table setting. And, the paisley-print table runners are the perfect foil for the red and white earthenware dinnerware.

Using What You Have

Good food management starts with the creative use of leftovers. Good flower management follows the same principles. Even if you have nurtured an arrangement with tender loving care, some of the flowers are going to fade before others. So, use the remaining blooms inventively. The second time around can be just as dramatic and exciting as the initial arrangement.

Classic Japanese flower arrangements, studied for years by Orientals, are ideal models for any homemaker who wants to make the most of few flowers. To an Oriental, these arrangements are the embodiment of high forms of philosophy, with each element rich in symbolism based on Nature's laws. As you learn the basic structural lines, it becomes easier and quicker to secure pleasing flower arrangements (whether you have 3 or 100 flowers to use).

The basic shape is an irregular triangle created by three basic stems that should form the structure of every well-balanced arrangement. The tallest stem, which you place first in your holder, is called 'heaven.' It can curve or undulate, but its tip should always be over its base. This stem is cut from 1½ to 3 times the width of your low bowl or above the rim of a high vase. The second structural line is called 'man.' It should reach ⅔ the height of heaven, the main stem. Place it in your flower holder so it slants toward your right or left shoulder. The third structural line is called 'earth' and is cut ⅓ the height of heaven line. It is placed to slant opposite the 'man.' Thus, you have a triangle that becomes the basic structure of your arrangement. All other flowers, branches, and leaves used in your arrangement are called 'helpers.' Select these specifically for each of the main heaven, man, and earth

A cast-iron caldron, a remnant or a reproduction from pioneer days, makes an unusual centerpiece container for a modern countrified table. Leaves, grapes, and bananas relieve the rounded shapes of the multicolored fruit.

The container for this table is a pressed glass reproduction. Feathers and greenery have been combined in a freewheeling interpretation of the classic Japanese arrangement. Many attractive objects can be used in these centerpieces.

lines, being sure they are all cut at different lengths. This creates a feeling of depth, a three-dimensional quality that allows each flower and branch to show its individual beauty to the utmost.

To keep your flowers looking fresh and growing, be sure to place them on the holder so each one faces up toward heaven line, just as they grow facing the sun. If you have only three flowers or branches, you place heaven, man, and earth close together on your holder. If you wish to make a larger arrangement, place heaven, man, and earth lines farther apart, allowing plenty of room for your helpers that will be near each of the main structural lines. To hide the holders, you may use such fillers as low-growing foliage or tips of evergreen or some low-growing ferns.

Low round, oval, or rectangular bowls are most usable for the dining table. Try baking dishes, salad bowls, casual tumblers, berry baskets, or anything around the house that you have in multiples. Also consider containers in graduated shapes, such as mixing bowls. These give a stepped feeling and are easy to use. And it is best to remember that the arrangement should not be so tall or massive as to restrict the flow of conversation. The general rule is to have the tallest flower or branch in your arrangement no longer than 14 inches if it is to be used in the center of the table. A very tall arrangement is most dramatic when placed at one end of the table, seating guests on the other three sides.

When making matching arrangements, always work on all of them at the same time. Put the outline flowers in each container first, checking that they look similar. Then, add the blooms that are second in importance. Finally, fill in with greenery or smaller flowers to flesh out the arrangements. View from all sides for balance.

Here, two arrangements of seemingly incompatible garden flowers are used together. Unity is achieved by matching greenery and the figurines. Place such groupings on trays, stands, or place mats to draw them together.

To fill a table, use a raised container and fill it with flowers whose main movement is horizontal. Fuchsias are particularly suited to horizontal use, since the flowers hang downward. Hide the rim by placing flowers low.

Accent With Table Decorations

Every meal is more enjoyable when you take time to make the table inviting. Even if you change the dining location, such as having breakfast in the kitchen and dinner in the dining area, a humdrum sameness can settle over meals like a curtain.

Use simple steps to make your mealtime transformations. You will find it is more enjoyable in the long run to accompany each meal with some type of table decoration. Saving all your efforts for occasional lavish displays dooms your family to boredom during the days in between.

One trick is to have a few centerpiece possibilities attractively decorating other areas in the home. Rotate these on the table. A centerpiece that is constantly on the table, no matter how beautiful, soon becomes dull. You stop really seeing it.

Keep long-lasting articles on hand that you can use at the table whenever you wish. Dried flowers or artificial fruits and flowers are ideal for this purpose.

Indoor plants are easy to rotate, and usually require it from time to time. Bring to the table only those that are in their prime, and retire others to a sun-drenched windowsill or a gardening area.

Plan ahead for wintertime arrangements, too. A wealth of dried, semipermanent materials is available in the fall. Buy them when they are most plentiful and use them all winter long. Good fall gathering includes gourds, Indian corn, dried flowers, and weeds and leaves. Catch the latter yourself and preserve them for use during the dreary days when not a leaf is in sight. They will warm the soul during the winter.

Remember also to suit decorations to the decor. Consider the entire feeling of a room. Is it traditional? Mediterranean? Early American? Modern? Study the kinds of centerpieces that were used during the periods when the furniture was first introduced. Often, they are the most compatible. It is very important that table decorations for sit-down meals are harmonious. Let them stimulate, but not be jarring.

Gaily colored, spray-painted containers on a paint-dressed tray form an artistic arrangement. A lush fern, with its forest coolness, is one of many houseplants that can be used within this same arrangement. Potted plants are ideal decorations for warm, sunny rooms.

Ornate candlestick holders are perfectly in context with the Mediterranean furnishings of this table setting. Candle and holder heights keep flames above eye level. A flat arrangement of tangerines and pears in a giant-size platter is good contrast to the dark table.

And don't forget to change your table covering and decorations to suit the season, just as you might with slipcovers. During the summer, increase the amount of greenery you use. In bright, overly sunny rooms, they will have a cooling effect. Choose cool colors—lavenders, blues, whites, greens, bluish pinks, or purples—for summer settings. Monochromatic schemes—tints and shades of one hue—are most stately and serene, and consequently seem the coolest.

Try primary pastel arrangements of the same hue, with accents of perhaps one stronger color. The foliage may be enough to give the form and zip you need.

Warm up winter dining areas with decorations made in hot colors and earth tones. Reds, golds, browns, beiges, and blackish browns, the usual colors of dried flowers, all make tables warm and inviting.

It is hard to conceive of garishly colored flowers, or garish floral arrangements. Use bright, strong, warm colors fearlessly in the fall and winter. The tension of a brilliant, strongly colored centerpiece is in itself warming to the eye and heart.

You must also consider the lighting. A deep red bouquet placed on a dark wood table with dim candlelight would be most effective. Check the lighting that you will be using before choosing centerpiece colors. Generally, it is best to pick warm colors for candlelight dining. Light colors show best, but if you want to use dark colors, highlight the arrangement by using accents of white. Pick white accented leaves, or anchor the flowers in a paper doily.

When choosing flowers, keep in mind your tablecloth or a matching napkin. Check for contrast as well as color harmony.

Quick-to-Make Decorations

All it takes is a brief phone call from your husband that he is bringing one or more business associates home with him, and suddenly, you're faced with entertaining unexpected guests for dinner. The food presents no problem that a quick trip to the supermarket won't solve, and the house can be straightened up in just a short time. But, the next step is a crucial one—how are you going to decorate the dining table on such short notice? This happens to the best of homemakers, and it's a compliment to your homemaking skills that your husband wants to entertain his friends at home. Don't despair. Use some of the following tricks to get the creative juices going again.

This buffet table is decorated with a burlap tablecloth and a basket of vegetables. The arresting display of textures in rustic natural touches includes the strong patterning of a country basket. Plastic foam anchors the carrots.

Look at your collection of containers. Then, free your imagination and see what comes to mind. Often, the container itself will suggest a certain type of centerpiece.

If you have your own flower garden, scrutinize it with an eagle eye for its best blooms. You can use these as a basis for your floral centerpiece arrangement. If necessary, you can buy a few flowers from your florist to fill any voids. Cut contrasting foliage from your houseplants. These make stunning arrangements and are handsome foils for any pattern of dinnerware.

Start with your favorite colors, and create a floral centerpiece that features a monochromatic color scheme. When you choose a one-color arrangement, you can make use of the slight variations in tone inherent in flower colors. Add interest by combining contrasting flower shapes, textures, and sizes. You may want to match the shades as nearly as possible, or you may wish to use gradations that vary from very deep shades to the lightest tints. Although these are called one-color arrangements, they are actually two-color because there is always green interspersed with the blooms.

Easy, spring, one-color arrangements team pink hyacinth, dogwood, and tulips. Or, you can combine daffodils with yellow tulips, daisies, and roses. Color-match various kinds of mums for fall.

Here again, the supermarket can be the source of many exciting decorations. Vegetables can be used alone, or with fruits and flowers. Save these arrangements for casual table settings, as the strong shapes of most vegetables would overwhelm highly ornate china and crystal.

Contrast green leaves and solid shapes to give greatest variety to your selection. Pick produce that is in its prime, and soak those items that need it, such as lettuce, celery, and carrots. Make your arrangement before the party, and refrigerate it until it is time to set the table.

Positioning of the produce is usually sufficient for low, horizontal arrangements. Secure taller arrangements with the same holders you use for flowers. Place vegetables into Oasis blocks. Anchor them with floral picks or toothpicks. Florist's clay will se-

This miniature rustic oxcart is loaded down with spring plants. Transitional material interspersed gives form to the centerpiece harmony.

A Victorian decorated china threesome, once at home on a washstand, becomes a centerpiece when it holds flowers, foliage, and mints.

cure eggs. Make matching candleholders from cored potatoes, artichokes, squash, onions, and eggplants.

One way of saving on the cost of flowers is to use containers with strong character. Often, less foliage is needed to complement them. Choose several with bright colors, strong patterns, or distinctive shapes.

Use florist's wire netting at the mouth of large containers, and fill them with less expensive flowers that are short stemmed. Salvage flowers cut or broken close to the blossom by floating them in a flat bowl filled with clear water. The trick is to support them on a platform of foamed plastic, potter's clay, or a tiny pin holder. Add twigs or leaves if a single bloom looks too lonely.

Making a center arrangement look optically larger is easy. Accessorize it with figurines or other objects that relate well to the container. Make miniature satellite bouquets to surround it. Around a center vase of glass, use glass tumblers. Fill them with leftover flowers and greenery.

To personalize a table, put small bouquets at each place setting. Keep them large enough in scale so that the total effect is not diffused. Single flowers are effective, too. Large blooms with a bit of foliage can be put into any small container. Use matched ones or a collection of unique pieces such as small baskets, bonbon dishes, or mini-vases. Place an individual, long-lasting bloom on each napkin, or fold the napkin so that it becomes a holder. Or, make miniature nosegays and boutonnieres for each place as fanciful as you like with tapered stems and pins.

Extend a centerpiece by using streamers radiating from it. Match the color of the streamers to the main flowers, in satin ribbons, crepe paper, or even pinked, patterned fabric. Or use flat greenery such as fern leaves. You might even try a minimum of flowers on a massive candlestick. Buy candle cups to place at the candle base, and fill them with flowers, too. With a candelabra, this may be enough.

The theme is green for a centerpiece that uses ferns and an evergreen sprig for foliage. A Japanese feeling is maintained with the use of a rimmed tray to contain the still life.

Heavenly heather spires repeat the graceful curves of a gleaming pewter pitcher. Bunched mums give the arrangement fullness at the rim. The heather tone is perfect with pewter.

Pin holders used to hold a nesting bunch of raffia mushrooms for a small centerpiece are in perfect character with the table setting.

Underpinnings Make It Easy

A wardrobe of flower holders is almost as essential to flower arranging as a variety of containers. No professional arrangers would be without them, and neither should you. Invest in a selection of holders as soon as possible. Most last a lifetime and pay for themselves many times over.

Needlepoint holders in a variety of shapes and sizes are essential in arranging flowers and foliage. This includes some of the heavier holders that do not tip over even when they are used to hold tall branches. If you are using a large container, use more than one holder in the bottom. Twigs and branches with their ends cut on a slant can be anchored easily on the larger, weighted needlepoint holders, whether you want them in an upright position or at an angle.

Florist's wire net, which is often coated with green plastic, is usable for deep containers or those that have unusual shapes.

Flowers in a container such as this need no support. The upright lines of the oriental pewter vase become serene when complemented by the graceful arches of slender leaves.

The last blooms of stately gold gladiolus are elegantly arranged in a pewter gravy boat with saucer. Because the blooms are sufficiently beautiful, they need no accessorizing.

Cut a large enough piece to make a loose mound in the bottom of the container.

Very fine green florist's wire is useful for arching and lengthening stems. As you wrap it around the stem, attach a toothpick or florist's pick to the end of the stem. It will be easier to anchor the stem in the plastic foam. Or, support slender stalks with thin twigs by splicing them and wrapping them with green floral tape.

A non-wire underpinning, plastic foam is a modern miracle worker. The soft variety, is easy to insert stems into, when it is well soaked with water. It also helps to keep the flowers fresh. When used inside containers, plastic foam can be repacked and reused a great many times.

Both florist's wire netting and plastic foam make good bases for global or cylindrical floral arrangements, with the foam being the best choice for an arrangement of fruits and vegetables. Use florist's clay or floral picks for extra anchoring of fruits and vegetables if you need to keep them in place securely.

Waterproof floral clay is invaluable for anchoring needlepoint holders firmly to the bottom of the container when you're arranging material with tall, heavy stems that might otherwise topple over.

The shape, size, and color of the flower container is of prime importance. Until you have gained experience in collecting bowls and vases, shun those that are bright in color, and strikingly patterned.

And while talking of equipment, invest in flower shears. A sharp knife is dangerous, and is less satisfactory for woody stems and branches. If you invest in a good set of tools, you can treat yourself to a Japanese flower arranger's kit that includes several cutting instruments specially designed for cutting and sawing woody stems.

Eventually, as you become more proficient at flower arranging, you'll probably want a special storage cabinet for your equipment.

Special-Occasion Entertaining

Special-occasion entertaining is what you make it. To some people it is a traditional event—Christmas, Easter, Thanksgiving, Valentine's Day, birthday, or anniversary. While for others, it's an infrequent event.

Probably the most popular form of entertaining is the birthday party. For youngsters, this is an eagerly anticipated event—an annual celebration that calls for ice cream and cake, games to suit the age group, and festive decorations. Even adults, who realize that a birthday makes them older, enjoy being honored.

One way to categorize special-occasion entertaining is to separate the events into annual, once-in-a-lifetime, and infrequent occurrences.

Annual events include religious holidays such as Christmas, Easter, Rosh Hashanah, Yom Kippur, Hanukkah, and Passover. These events

and Thanksgiving are more or less family get-togethers. New Year's and Halloween are other holidays that are celebrated with parties that are more casual and with many guests.

There are other annual events to celebrate besides official holidays—birthdays and anniversaries.

Once-in-a-lifetime occasions include weddings, wedding showers, and bachelor dinners. Then, there are baby showers, christenings, confirmations and Bar Mitzvahs, and graduations. These range from small gatherings to large, elaborate parties.

The list of infrequent events that foster a celebration is as varied as it is lengthy—housewarming, farewell, bon voyage, promotion, and retirement parties. It is also thoughtful to honor those who have achieved a certain degree of accomplishment—winners in bridge tournaments, sailing races, or tennis tournaments, for example. Then there are brunches before football games, or parties afterward, and late suppers after skiing or ice skating, concerts, ballets, or the theater. Each is a special occasion that calls for a party.

← *For an informal snack in front of the fireplace, combine a wood salad bowl overflowing with cheese and fruit, breadsticks and crackers, goblets and wine, plates, and napkins in a rack.*

Birthdays, Anniversaries, Weddings, and Showers

Entertaining for any special occasion—unless it is a strictly formal affair—has become more relaxed and casual than ever before. This includes birthdays and anniversaries that can be celebrated every year, or weddings and showers, those memorable once-in-a-lifetime occasions that justly deserve the 'red carpet' treatment.

This doesn't mean that the style has gone out of entertaining. On the contrary, with a relaxed style, you have more freedom to make festive events even more joyous occasions for the guest of honor and the guests, and at the same time, enjoy yourself just as much as they do. As long as you stay within the general guidelines dictated by good taste and manners, you can give vent to all your creative instincts.

Birthday Parties

You don't have to be seven years old—and invite your little friends to share ice cream and cake, paper hats, and favors—in order to enjoy birthdays. They can be just as much fun for adults as they are for children if you select the menu with care, make sure the food is delectable, and gear the table settings and decorations to the overall festive spirit that prevails.

Even those who are in that dreaded age group between 40 and 80—past the youthful age, and before reaching the distinguished pinnacle of claiming the ripe old age of four score—will appreciate being honored one day each year. Just be sure you plan all the details with the likes and dislikes

This gypsy-inspired birthday party, which features a gypsy-skirt tablecloth, mix-and-match plastic dinnerware and tumblers, and stainless flatware, bounces with color. Even the tomatoes, strawberries, marshmallows, and cake icing hold their own against the cloth.

of the guest of honor in mind rather than your own personal preferences. There are those who prefer small, intimate dinners with family members or close friends. Some like buffets or cocktail parties with many guests. And, there are still others who have picnics and patio parties at the top of their list. Once you've decided on the type of party, plan the menu with your guest of honor's favorite foods in mind.

Equally as important as the food served are the table settings and table decorations. This is your chance to be as inventive as your talents, time, and budget will allow. Establish a theme for the table decorations around the guest of honor's special interests, hobbies, or occupation.

For a golfer, incorporate golf balls and tees into the centerpiece decorations, and present them to the 'Arnie Palmer' hopeful as a birthday gift when the party is over.

If the guest of honor is an avid follower of the stock market, make place mats out of the financial section of the newspaper, and a papier mache bull and bear resting in a nest of ticker tape for a centerpiece.

For a woman who is a knitting enthusiast, feature the 'knit and purl' theme by making a centerpiece for the table in the style of a floral arrangement, except use balls of yarn and knitting needles instead of flowers and foliage. Use some of the yarn to tie around napkins instead of using napkin rings. If a gift is in order, make it a handsome knitting bag.

If the honoree, either male or female, dotes on gourmet cookery, decorate the table with a centerpiece composed of gourmet cookware items. Shop in your favorite houseware department or import shop for items such as a flan pan, wire whip, butter mold, garlic press, pepper mill, individual soufflé dishes, crepe pan, fish poacher, quiche pan, pancake iron, and butter curler. Purchase several that can form a cohesive centerpiece and intersperse a few flowers to add color. At the end of the evening, present the centerpiece to the celebrant.

These are only a few suggestions for themes. You can dream up your own—just be sure to link it to the guest of honor's interests and the total table setting.

When you celebrate a silver wedding anniversary, you want everything to be very elegant. The centerpiece above rises to the occasion—an arrangement of roses in a container that doubles as candelabra. You can even rent containers like this from your local florist.

Anniversaries

Anniversary celebrations are, without a doubt, the most sentimental of all entertaining occasions. They range all the way from an intimate dinner for two for the anniversary couple to a large and lavish reception for many relatives and friends. A rule of thumb for anniversary entertaining is that entertaining for the early years can be as informal and casual as you like. But, when it comes to the major anniversaries—the 25th, 50th, and 75th—make them as elaborate as possible.

Anniversary parties can take the form of a sit-down dinner, a buffet dinner, a cocktail party, or a tea or reception. They may be given by the anniversary couple themselves, or they may be planned and hosted by close friends or relatives who wish to surprise the honored guests on this extra-special day. If the weatherman cooperates with your plans, this is an ideal occasion for entertaining outdoors—either on the lawn or the patio, or at poolside.

A 50th or 75th anniversary celebration is almost always hosted by the honored couple's children. If you're in charge of the preparations, set an elegant anniversary tea or buffet table with dainty sandwiches, mints and nuts, a beautifully decorated cake, and beverages. Use fine china, sterling flatware, and beautiful table linens.

When giving such a party, be sure to provide comfortable seating for your guests of honor since the hours are usually long.

The anniversary symbols are provided by tradition. These are natural aids for table decorations and centerpieces, and for gifts. The following table lists the traditional symbol for the special years.

The blue and white tableware in the picture below takes its cue from the totally coordinated floral decorations. Extra touches, such as the Star of David made of ribbon on the table, show that this Bar Mitzvah has been planned with care. Without the Star of David, the same table appointments and table decorations would be suitable for a wedding brunch.

Anniversary Themes

1. Paper	13. Lace
2. Cotton	14. Ivory
3. Leather	15. Crystal
4. Fruit and flowers	20. China
5. Wood	25. Silver
6. Sugar and candy	30. Pearl
7. Wool or copper	35. Coral
8. Bronze or pottery	40. Ruby
9. Willow or pottery	45. Sapphire
10. Tin or aluminum	50. Gold
11. Steel	60. Emerald
12. Silk or linen	75. Diamond

Weddings

Make a wedding reception the happiest occasion of all celebrations. In order for everyone to enjoy it to the utmost—including the mother of the bride—plan in advance for every detail. Study a wedding guide book, or hire a bridal consultant to help you make your reception plans.

If the reception is to be held in a club or a hotel reception room, your responsibilities will be limited to choosing the menu and working with the florist in selecting the decorations.

However, the degree of elaborateness depends on the time of day of the wedding service. If it is a morning wedding, follow it with a wedding breakfast—either a buffet or a sit-down meal. For an afternoon wedding, have a relatively simple reception. On the other hand, an evening wedding demands more formality and a lavish treatment.

But whichever type of reception you choose, be sure the table is beautifully set. Cover it with a plain white damask tablecloth and use white plates, or white with a gold or platinum border. White flowers generally are used for centerpieces, but there may be exceptions if the entire wedding is geared to a definite color scheme. For example, a wedding that takes place on or near Christmas or Valentine's Day may have a red and white theme; an autumn wedding may feature the bronze tones of fall.

Regardless of how simple or lavish the menu is, champagne is the accepted beverage for weddings. This is a tradition that makes it possible for the guests to drink a toast to the newlyweds' health and future. For those who do not wish to drink alcohol, substitute a fruit punch.

Showers

If you took a survey, you'd probably come up with the statistics that almost every female over 18 has been to one or more showers—and that a large majority of them have hosted one or more. You might also find that most of them have followed the same humdrum procedure—cake, ice cream, and beverages; inane games; and a long, drawn-out period of time devoted to the gift-opening process by the bride-to-be.

So, the next time you have occasion to give a shower, take it out of the stereotyped class and make it something special.

Before outlining the suggestions for giving showers a 'new look,' it might be well to list a few 'dos' and 'don'ts' that apply to wedding showers in general.

1. Two or possibly three showers are enough for any one person. When it goes beyond this, it is a burden on those who seem to receive invitations to all of the showers. If several showers are already planned and you still wish to entertain for the bride-to-be, host a breakfast or brunch or a bridge luncheon—without gifts.

2. Bridal showers should never be given by members of the bride's or groom's immediate family, as a gift is obligatory.

3. Clear the date with the guest of honor first, and then phone or mail invitations 10 days to two weeks in advance.

4. Confine the guest list to close friends and relatives of the guest of honor. Never feel obligated to invite your friends—you can always entertain them another time.

5. If the newlyweds will be living in a distant location, avoid gifts that are fragile or cumbersome to pack and transport. It's much easier to pack linens and lingerie than an ironing board or punch bowl.

The theme for a bridal shower can stem from the bride-to-be's favorite color and her needs for the new home she is furnishing. After you choose the theme, be sure to carry it through in table decorations and centerpiece, tableware, and refreshments.

Linen showers can be a real joy because you don't have to be concerned about a duplication of gifts—whoever heard of anyone having too many sheets or towels?

Find out first what decorating scheme the guest of honor plans for her new home, and inform the guests in advance so they can choose appropriate colors when they purchase their shower gifts. Carry out the theme and the color scheme by creating a centerpiece out of fingertip towels rolled and folded to simulate live blooms and intersperse with foliage or dried materials. This can be your gift to the honoree.

Even paper, mundane as it sounds, offers unlimited possibilities as a theme for a shower. Gifts can include anything from cookbooks to fine etchings or prints. Decorate the table with paper items—papier mache figures of a bridal couple, mobiles, or flowers. And set the table with paper plates, cups, napkins, and tablecloth or mats.

Pronunciation Guide

White Dinner Wines

Chablis	sha-blee'
Pinot Chardonnay	pea-no shar-doh-nay'
Pinot Blanc	pea-no blanh
Chenin Blanc	she-nahn blahn
Sauterne	so-tairn'
Sauvignon Blanc	so-vee-nyonh blanh
Semillon	say'-mee'yonh
Riesling	reez'-ling
Sylvaner	sil'-vah'ner
Traminer	trah-mee'-ner

Red Dinner Wines

Charbono	shar-bo-no
Gamay	gah-may
Pinot Noir	pea-no no-ohr
Red Pinot	red pea-no
Cabernet Sauvignon	kab-er-nay' so-vee-nyonh
Zinfandel	zin-fan-dell
Gamay Beaujolais	gah-may boh-sho-lay

Themes for Entertaining

It's like that old story, 'which came first, the chicken or the egg?' Only in this case, it's 'which comes first, the party or the theme?' For example, some people plan months ahead to have a Christmas open house. There's no problem picking a theme, as the holiday itself dictates the theme. Others plan an impromptu party for the following Saturday night—and then hurriedly search for an appropriate theme. It doesn't really matter which approach you take because there are enough different themes for entertaining for all 365 days of the year. And, if it happens to be that one year in four when there are 366 days, you can host a Leap Year party on February 29.

There are holidays that are celebrated nationwide that have a built-in theme as well as calling for a definite color scheme. Christmas, New Year's, Valentine's Day, St. Patrick's, Easter, Memorial Day, Fourth of July, Halloween, and Thanksgiving all fall in this particular category.

But don't stop there. There are many lesser-known dates that also can spark a party and be a great deal of fun if you put

A New Year's Eve party is an ideal showplace for you to demonstrate to your friends that it isn't what flowers you use for a centerpiece, but how you put them together. Here, flowers are combined with balloons and streamers to create a matchless holiday mood.*

Traditional red and green are always a good choice for Christmas decorations. The red carnations, candles, and apples combined with green boughs and checked ribbons add up to a happy decorating scheme. Add to this trays of Christmas cookies and a silver punch bowl of holiday eggnog and you have all the fixings for an open house for a large crowd.

your imagination to work. For example, there's Bastille Day, Bunker Hill Day, Texas Independence Day, Derby Day, Elias Howe's birthday (he invented the sewing machine), and Daffodil Day in Puyallup, Washington. You can probably think of many more.

Also, there are dates set aside to promote a product or a service, such as National Pickle Week or National Bourbon Month.

Those who travel extensively have still another source for themes for entertaining. Build a theme around New England clam chowder, exotic Hawaiian cuisine, a south-of-the-border menu, a Scandinavian smorgasbord, or an oriental feast. For these occasions, the food itself usually sets the theme,

and mementoes you have collected on your trips can be used in centerpieces and table decorations to enhance the theme.

Then there are those occasions when you entertain before or after an athletic event, or a musical or dramatic production.

It's up to you to decide just which type of entertaining you enjoy the most, and no matter which day of the year you wish to host a party, you'll find there's something noteworthy that will suggest a theme.

Southern Hospitality

A plantation breakfast (or hunt breakfast) has long been a popular form of entertaining in Virginia. And, even though you may not live in Virginia and you and your friends don't 'ride to the hounds' prior to this hearty midday breakfast or brunch, inject the true flavor of the old South with traditional foods, beverages, and decorations.

Set the table buffet-style, and place the punch bowl and coffee service on a nearby table. Let the guests serve themselves.

Decorate the table with floral and fauna arrangements of boxwood, osage oranges, pyracantha, magnolias, and Spanish moss. If you can't get these materials from your florist, invest in some of the natural-looking permanent forms and use them many times.

Draw on the rich heritage of the South by using any antique china, silver, glassware and pewter that you may have.

To further the theme, ask your guests to come dressed for a hunt. This theme is especially appropriate for the day of the Kentucky Derby, the Preakness, or Belmont races. Watching the race on TV with friends is the next best thing to being there.

Your hunt breakfast will long be remembered if you serve a variety of southern foods and beverages. There are so many to choose from—shrimp, mint juleps, southern ham and fried chicken, biscuits, spoon bread, grits and gravy, watermelon pickles, sliced fresh tomatoes, mushrooms and watercress in sour cream served on toast, ambrosia, scrambled eggs, and hot sausage.

Create a bit of nostalgia and relive the southern plantation days with a bountiful repast and harmonious decorations.

"May the luck of the Irish be with you" when you plan a St. Patrick's Day buffet. Here, a pyramid of limes and lemon blossoms is flanked by silver candelabra with white tapers, stalks of bells of Ireland, and lemon blossoms. Use your best china, flatware, crystal, and linens.

A Little Bit of Sweden

The smorgasbord, a Swedish buffet luncheon or supper, is the perfect theme for entertaining a large group of friends.

For the buffet table centerpiece, laden a Viking ship replica with flowers. Add other Swedish decorations—hang tapestries, straw animals, and posters around your room—and fill Swedish glassware containers with floral bouquets. If you don't already have these accessories, you can find them at Scandinavian import shops.

Traditional smorgasbord fare includes hors d'oeuvres, hot and cold meats, smoked and pickled fish, sausages, cheeses, salads, relishes, homemade bread and rolls, and a variety of delicate and hearty pastries. The smorgasbord is, undoubtedly, the best-known presentation of Swedish food.

Seat your guests at small tables covered with two tablecloths—one that is floor-length. On top of this, put a smaller square cloth with a brightly colored border.

The Exotic Luau

No longer is the luau confined to the tropical islands that comprise the state of Hawaii. People everywhere have adopted this colorful theme for entertaining.

This is a style of entertaining that lends itself to buffet-style. Instead of a tablecloth, cover the entire tabletop with a layer of ti leaves. In the center of the table, place a large arrangement of tropical fruit, anthurium, and ti leaves. Ask your guests to come attired in luau shirts and muu muus, and be sure to greet each guest by placing a lei—either of paper or inexpensive flowers—around his/her neck.

Hawaiian cuisine is a mixture of Chinese, Japanese, Filipino, Korean, Portuguese, and American specialties, and, of course, the Pacific Islands. It is actually a variety of dishes from various countries.

The food at a luau is hearty and plentiful. The highlight of the meal usually is a roasted suckling pig. Other meat dishes such as barbecued spareribs and baked ham, fish and seafood, several salads, and vegetables also are part of the traditional luau menu. Add to this punch that is made from a blend of tropical fruit juices, and tropical fruits for dessert and you have a meal that will whet the most jaded appetites.

After everyone has feasted to their hearts' content, the luau entertainment begins. In tune with the luau theme, this usually consists of Hawaiian music and hula dancing.

South of the Border

There's nothing more colorful than a fiesta theme borrowed from our Mexican neighbors. Adapt this theme either to indoor or outdoor entertaining.

Create a vivid color scheme that is inherent to the Mexican way of life. Cover the table with gaily striped table runners or place mats, and decorate it with ornate candelabra and a centerpiece made of brilliantly colored flowers. Hang a serape on one wall, and use pinatas as decorative accessories elsewhere in the room. Set the table with pottery dinnerware, tinware, and jewel-colored glassware.

Mexican cookery is a conglomerate of dishes and cooking methods that have been handed down by many generations of Mexicans blended with dishes that were introduced by the Spanish and others. This cuisine is characterized by spicy foods.

Take your guests on a south-of-the-border food trip by serving tortillas, tacos, enchiladas, tamales, and re-fried beans. Although beef and pork are Mexican favorites, other meats, poultry, fish, and eggs are also used to add variety. For dessert, choose a creamy custard or pudding to soothe the tongue from the bite of fiery foods.

A large basket with a profusion of zinnia, mum, and marigold blooms picks up the colors of the pinata and ornate candelabra that are typical of Mexican handcrafted items. The table runner, napkins, napkin rings, and patterned dinnerware repeat the same colors.

Bon Voyage

Give your traveling friends a happy send-off with a bon voyage party, especially if they are people who rarely take long trips. A trip to a faraway place is exciting and romantic to those who rarely leave home, and the honor of being entertained at a going-away party will make it even more exciting.

Begin your party plans by consulting the guests of honor. Only a very well organized family would think it fun to have the send-off the night before their departure. Most people would prefer the less-hectic time of several days before. So it's best to ask what fits into their schedule best.

For entertaining of this type you can make your own clever invitations, using your honored guests' destination as the motif. Or phone or write informal notes.

A bon voyage party can be a brunch, a luncheon, sit-down or buffet dinner, or a cocktail party. Make the guest list as long as you wish. Just be sure that those you invite all know the guests of honor well.

Use your imagination and skill to dream up an unusual centerpiece for the table. If the guests of honor are heading for Alaska, make an igloo of papier mache, place it on a snow-white mat, and surround it with small figures of polar bears. If their destination is Hawaii, combine tropical fruits and exotic blooms in a handwoven basket, and surround it with sea shells. For those who are heading for Africa, create your own jungle-like safari theme. Enhance it by hanging travel posters on the walls.

When you plan the menu, be sure to include at least one or two dishes whose origins are the area that will be traveled.

Gifts for the guests of honor are in order at a bon voyage party. Select those items that travel well and that they don't already have. Travel sizes of cologne, cosmetics, or grooming aids in lightweight plastic containers are always handy. Consider also a foreign language paperback dictionary, an electric razor adaptor, guidebooks, and packaged wet towels. Don't load them down with bulky or heavy items. This only adds to the last-minute confusion, and makes packing and traveling difficult.

Housewarming

A housewarming is a friendly way to say "welcome to the neighborhood" to new arrivals. Friends and neighbors reverse the traditional role and become hosts in the newcomers' new home. It can be the night they move in, or it can be later when they're more settled. Whenever you plan to have it, a surprise party is in order.

Since the newcomers will not be settled, perhaps not even unpacked, the guests bring the edibles—sandwiches, liquids in vacuum containers, casseroles in electric containers, and trays of relishes and snacks. Also, bring along disposable plates, cups, utensils, napkins, and table covers. Be sure that someone brings an ice bucket, ice, and a bottle opener. Gifts are not mandatory, but it is nice to give the newcomers something for their new home.

April Fool's Day

You may not think of April Fool's Day as a theme for a party, but it does provide endless possibilities for party ideas. Use this excuse to welcome April and spring by inviting friends to a luncheon or dinner.

You can mix-and-match to your heart's content for your April Fool's Day prank. Use as many china or pottery and silver patterns as you have available—use a different one at each place setting if this is possible. Cover the table with your wildest tablecloth and use a different color napkin at each place. Have an unconventional centerpiece—dead branches instead of flowers, and fireplace matches inserted into foam plastic holders instead of candles.

Although the menu should be appealing, make it unconventional, too. Try one of those special recipes that you've been saving for just the right occasion.

If you're planning an evening of entertainment, throw in a few children's party games to play for a novel touch. Mind-teasing games are appropriate for April Fool's Day. Divide your guests into teams for some friendly competition. Even Old Maid will provide a humorous children's touch for a congenial group of adults.

This Sunday brunch, planned for four in a suburban setting, has overtones of affluence in fine china, crystal, and silver flatware and serving pieces. Favorite sculptured pieces share the honors as a combined centerpiece—resting on an ebony platform. The napkins are handmade, tone-on-tone strips, each one in a different color. With the new freedom of style in contemporary entertaining, the Sunday brunch has become a favorite with hostesses.

Theater Supper Party

Entertaining a group of your friends at a late supper after an evening at the theater provides a grand finale to a gala event.

Although a supper party appears to have an easy, casual air about it, there should be an aura of elegance. Use some flowers and candles for your table centerpiece, and inventively incorporate theater programs into your table decorations.

The number of guests you invite is up to you. You can invite more than you would to a sit-down dinner, for seating is no problem. Guests won't mind sitting on the floor.

Even though a supper party appears to be delightfully spontaneous, it does require advance planning if you want to enjoy the evening and still be a gracious hostess.

Whatever you plan for your menu, prepare it ahead of time. Plan easy-to-eat foods that can be placed on a buffet or table and kept warm. Use warming trays and chafing dishes to keep foods at the right temperature. When the guests arrive, serve drinks immediately. While they are enjoying their drinks and conversation, you can complete your final food preparation and serving chores. Because of the late hour, guests will want to eat as soon as possible, so try to serve within a half hour.

Good conversation is the only entertainment necessary for a supper party. Most everyone will have opinions about the event they have just attended, and this should trigger some lively debates. If you wish to have background music, keep it low so that it doesn't disturb conversation.

Oriental Theme

The cool serenity of oriental dining is easily achieved by American hostesses who take their legends to heart and follow customs to create a Far Eastern theme. With the continually mounting interest in all things of oriental design or origin, there is a wealth of accessories that are easy to make or to purchase at little cost.

Most novelty shops sell colorful, inexpensive imports from Hong Kong and Japan. You can use many of these as a springboard for your decorative theme. Large and miniature paper parasols, paper lanterns, paper wall scrolls, brightly colored rice bowls, chopsticks, and even paper kimonos and robes are relatively inexpensive and won't dent your budget.

Since oriental flower arrangements are rather austere, all you really need are several bud vases or tall, slender vases containing one or two blooms combined with foliage or dried materials. If you have a jade figure, an oriental vase, or a Foo dog, plan a centerpiece of your own design.

An overall oriental decorating theme is particularly successful outside in gardens or patios and in family rooms. So don't limit your party decorating or your party giving to the living and dining areas in your home. You can decorate all over the house when you use your imagination.

Even if you and your guests are not adept at using chopsticks, plan and prepare an oriental menu for your party. If you have dinnerware with an oriental pattern, this is the perfect time to show it off.

Bring a bit of the Orient into your home and create a Far East theme. Here, a white sampan on a bamboo 'raft' voyages with a cargo of yellow daffodils and is flanked by yellow candles in brass holders. Place china on bamboo mats, and chopsticks on knife-rests.

Here's a Taj Mahal table setting theme—concocted with the guile of an Indian fakir. The handsome tablecloth supplies the perfect background for brass bowls and the filigree tracery of fine china. The napkin rings are actually Indian toe rings. Add a bowl of exotic flowers.

Magic Carpet Trip

Take your guests on a magic carpet trip to the exotic East—destination: Persia. This is a land of fabled enchantment and mysteries as richly woven and colorful as the world-famous carpets that are made there.

Fashion your own invitations to simulate sultan-sized decrees. Make them from pieces of yellow cardboard or construction paper that measure about 8x12 inches. Write the request in your most flourishing handwriting on a smaller sheet of white paper, and fasten it to the sheet of yellow cardboard. Then affix your official seal—a bright sunburst flower cut from paper and decorated with gold ribbon streamers.

As your guests arrive, welcome them with a put-on favor to wear throughout the evening. Give the men brightly colored trailing sashes and the women bead necklaces. Make your own sashes from strips of cloth and trim them with gold braid or bits of broken jewelry. Make the necklaces by stringing plastic beads on gold cord, or buy some if you're pressed for time.

Capture Persia's opulent aura in your table setting. Start with an ornately patterned tablecloth that you can make from inexpensive cotton yard goods. Then add napkins that match the brightest color in the table cover. For a striking centerpiece, choose exotic blooms and foliage in colors that harmonize with the tablecloth and napkins. Or, for a non-floral centerpiece, fill a brass bowl with costume jewelry and let it cascade over the edges and onto the table.

For the final touch, round up anything brass, such as candlesticks and goblets, and some bowls in which to serve food.

With the guests already Persia-primed, it's time to partake of a feast fit for a shah. For the main dish, serve curried lamb, which can be spooned over mounds of fluffy rice flecked with raw carrots. Along with this, offer individual bowls of condiments: kumquats, mango chutney, sliced green onion, raisins, coconut, and peanuts. Complete the meal with *chapati*, the flat bread of India; add a fruit compote for dessert.

When you entertain, Persian-style, your guests will long remember the occasion.

Informal Entertaining

Informal entertaining encompasses all kinds of parties. They can be for special occasions or for no reason at all. They can be impromptu or planned ahead. As delightfully diverse as the people who host them, they all have the same purpose—to have fun. Whether they are for large or small groups, or indoors or outdoors, they can be as much fun to give as they are to go to. On the pages that follow you'll find a host of ideas for informal entertaining.

With more and more emphasis being directed toward informal and casual entertaining, hostesses are finding it easier to give parties. Menus and food are scaled-down, simplified, and easy to prepare and serve. With all the convenience foods available, and a streamlined kitchen in which to prepare them, the hostess has more time to devote to planning table settings, centerpieces, and decorations. These are the exciting things that turn entertaining from the 'have to' into the 'want to' category.

Buffets

If you conducted a survey, you'd probably find that the buffet is at the top of the list of most hostesses when it comes to informal entertaining. The advantages are numerous—you can entertain a larger group than is possible at a sit-down meal, you don't have to worry about a seating plan so last-minute additions or cancellations of guests won't alter plans, and there is a spontaneity generated by the fact that the group can mingle freely with each other.

Here are a few tips that will make buffet-style meals easier for you:

1. Prepare everything ahead so you will have a minimum of last-minute cooking.

2. Give your buffet table a festive look with a centerpiece and table decorations that are appropriate for the occasion.

3. To serve hot dishes, use warming trays, electric casseroles, and chafing dishes to keep food at serving temperature.

4. Provide a butter plate or small dish beside each hot serving dish so that guests will be less likely to leave the serving utensils in the casserole.

5. If you lack serving dishes, put your imagination to work and press unlikely items into service—canisters, ice buckets, punch bowls, even your electric skillet.

6. If there's someone to serve coffee at the buffet table, have it there. If not, put the coffee on a side table.

7. Do not place a dessert on the buffet table. It should either be on a side table or passed to the guests.

8. In order to have more room for serving dishes on the buffet table, arrange the dishes, flatware, and napkins on a sideboard.

Safety Tips

- If your centerpiece is made up of materials that include evergreen, paper, or dried materials, be sure to keep the candles a safe distance away from the inflammables so as to prevent the possibility of a fire starting in the room.
- Be sure that candles are firmly fixed in their holders, and use a bobeche on each candle holder to catch wax drippings. This will save much clean-up time.
- Many people are attracted to primitive or handcrafted ceramics, but lead poisoning can result if the common lead glaze is not properly handled. If you have any doubts, use the receptacle for decorative purposes only—not to hold food, especially those containing fruit juices or wine.
- If you have both smokers and non-smokers in your home, it's a good idea to have several lighted candles around the room. They help to clear the air of smoke. You can also buy specially treated candles that do this same job even more effectively.

Party With a Paintbrush

For the newcomers in the neighborhood, or those who are redecorating, host a party and lend a hand. This is definitely a party for those active people who enjoy puttering around the house—anyone's house! String cardboard invitations to a real paintbrush, and pass them out in the neighborhood. When the guests arrive, provide them with paper coveralls and rollers or brushes. Serve cold drinks from ice-filled buckets, and serve hearty sandwiches, an assortment of crisp relishes, and some snacks. Note of caution: cover furniture and floors well.

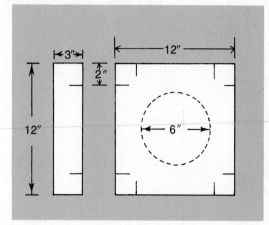

Make 1-inch-deep notches on squares 2 inches from each corner. Notch ends of strip in the same manner. Cover with adhesive-backed vinyl. Cut 6-inch circles in center of two squares. Use picture below as a guide.

The crafty creation below is a makeshift unit suitable for small buffet gatherings. Follow the diagram in the upper right-hand corner for cutting the pieces of corrugated cardboard. Cut six 12-inch squares and six 12x2-inch strips.

For an afternoon snack, set a small table with sterling silver and crystal wine goblets. Serve fruit, cheese and crackers, and wine.

Wine and Cheese

Wine-tasting parties have been around for a long time, but when you invite your friends to join you in a wine- and cheese-tasting party, you're bound to be voted in the winner of the 'hostess of the year' award.

This casual type of entertaining puts the emphasis exactly where it belongs—on the food and the beverages. Clear your coffee table, and place on it a tray of crackers, French bread, and rye bread; a cutting board with wedges of cheese arranged on it; and a few bottles of wine.

This appetizer/main course offers a rich variety of flavors—brie, edam, port du salut, crema danica, gruyere, gorgonzola, and la grappe cheeses. Add to this goblets of dry red wine, and no wonder the guests hover around the coffee table where they can reach out for the cheese and wine and compare taste reactions, without making disruptive trips to a buffet table.

Because cheese is so very rich and filling, keep the rest of the dinner light. Why not serve a tomato bisque with small pieces of avocado floating on top for color and flavor, decorative loaves of bread, and a delicious tossed salad with a dressing?

Another advantage to serving the wine and cheese from the coffee table is that it frees your dining table for buffet duty when it's mealtime. Actually, all you have to do is toss the salad and warm the soup.

Decorate the buffet table with clay pots of geraniums and foliage plants, and use your colorful plastic dinnerware.

For the finale, offer a sinfully rich torte piled with gobs of whipped cream. Serve it from a small circular table draped with a red tablecloth. No one will be able to resist this—even the calorie counters will have forgotten how to add by then.

Chuck Wagon Special

For your western barbecue party, try a chuck wagon special. Let your guests know the theme so they can dress casually.

Set up the chuck wagon table outdoors, or in the family room if the weatherman refuses to cooperate. Make the table of rough board planks set on sawhorses. Set the table with red bandana napkins, casual pottery dinnerware or patterned paper plates, iron pots for serving dishes, and a centerpiece of cactus. Use lanterns for light.

Keep your menu casual, too. The food should be substantial and a little on the spicy side. Serve generous portions of barbecued beef, pinto beans spooned over corn bread, a tossed green salad, and beverage.

If you have the room, this is a good time to try your hand at square dancing. You can buy records of square dance music, or you can find a local caller for the evening. If one of your friends has a guitar, ask him to bring it along and all of the songs of the Old West he can remember. This will get the evening off to a good start.

Garden Party

You'll want your garden to be in perfect shape if it's to be the center of attraction at a brunch, luncheon, or a dinner party. So be sure you've watered well at least four days ahead of time, trimmed out any weeds or dead flowers, sprayed with insecticides, swept the patio, and thoroughly cleaned all of the lawn furniture.

The daisy pattern dinnerware above holds its own with the floral printed tablecloth. The flatware, turquoise footed water goblets, yel- low napkins, and the delicate flower candles also complement the tablecloth. This is a per- fect setting for a small luncheon group.

Add to your theme with some extra touches—special lighting if it's to be an evening affair, outdoor floral arrangements, and brightly painted baskets to hold litter.

Carry your garden theme into your table setting, too. Repeat the flower colors, add a floral centerpiece, and serve a garden-fresh meal with greens and flower blossoms. The menu should be as light and airy as the setting. Serve a party salad of fresh vegetables and thinly sliced luncheon meat or seafood, or of fresh fruit and cottage cheese. Serve iced drinks, too.

You'll find a portable serving cart an invaluable aid at an outdoor garden party. Wheel out all at once all necessary utensils and all courses to save you making many trips in and out of the house.

Mariner's Sea Fare

Plan a mariner's party, even if you don't own a boat, large or small, or if you have to rent one for a day. Make it a take-along special. Take everything you need with you and enjoy a party at a particular scenic land site or on board the boat.

Unless you want a sea caravan of several boatloads of sailors who meet at the ap- pointed spot for their sea feast, plan the party for a small crowd, since you'll have to carry all of the food and beverages to the eventual destination.

The outdoor scenery provides the party decorations. All you need to furnish are the eating utensils, tablecloth, plates, cups— all disposable—a blanket or pillows for the guests to sit on, and the food. Don't forget to bring along the necessary extras—a bottle opener, a sharp knife, salt and pepper shakers, serving spoons, matches, a portable grill, if necessary, charcoal, paper, and some firewood.

Sailing and swimming will probably supply your main entertainment, but if you have an energetic gang with you, take along some sports equipment—beach balls, a la crosse set, a badminton set, or a croquet set. For the bridge fans in the group or if you're lunching on board the boat, include a few decks of playing cards. And for the ecology-minded, be very careful about disposing of the litter.

For the benefit of the landlubbers, make it known in advance that everyone is expected to wear rubber-soled shoes. And when they come aboard, show them where the life preservers are stored.

Potlucks

Potluck dinners have a reputation for being carefree, relaxing, and as much fun for the hostess as they are for the guests. You can even add to the guest list at the last minute without causing any confusion.

Although informal, they definitely are not 'spur of the moment.' You must plan in advance to have the right variety and amount of food. The best way is to have each guest bring her favorite in a category that you set up. For example, meat or vegetable dishes, relishes, salads, and desserts. To add an international flavor, ask each cook to bring a foreign dish—Swedish meatballs, Italian spaghetti, Danish torte, German potato salad, French bread, etc. However you obtain the menu, you must provide the condiments, rolls, and beverage.

Avoid most of the work of post-party clean-up chores by using paper plates, mugs, table covers, and napkins. Choose from the many exciting colors and designs.

If your potluck will be an outdoor affair and guests will bring refrigerated dishes, use insulated food servers to keep food chilled, or employ the family ice chest. If it's an indoor party, run a heavy-duty extension cord with several outlets to the buffet table. Then suggest that guests bring hot dishes in the electric skillet or casserole in which they were prepared. Have on hand an electric warming tray, too, for keeping things hot until they are needed.

If you need extra tables and chairs, rent them from a rental service at little cost.

Instead of planned entertainment, ask each couple to bring a bottle of wine (set a limit on the price), and ask them to remove the label from the bottle but identify the bottle by a number. As the guests sample the various types of wines, let them attempt to identify them by type (not by brand), and list the answers on a sheet of paper. Reward the one who has the longest and most correct list of answers with a prize—a bottle of wine.

Set up a line of snack tables, alternating place settings from right to left-hand side. This is a comfortable eating arrangement when you are entertaining a small group.

Stack some snacks on a three-tier pyramid— any novice handyman can make these. Use lowest part for eating, second for serving, top for decorations or more serving pieces.

The table setting for this fondue party is as colorful and picturesque as the food itself is. The table cover, dinnerware, and the fondue pot carry out a coordinated color scheme. There's a relaxed atmosphere to a fondue party because guests help with the cooking.

Tabletop Cooking

When you invite friends to a fondue party, you're certain of a lively fun-for-all. The food provides the entertainment here, with each guest dipping or cooking his own.

There are a few ground rules for a successful fondue party, although it's a casual meal that needs little preplanning on your part. Count on only four people serving themselves from each pot—probably the biggest job you will have is rounding up enough fondue pots and electric saucepans for everyone. For a good-sized group, set up small tables—card or coffee tables are fine—and outfit each one with a heating unit, fondue forks, plates, napkins, and, of course, the featured food.

A cheese fondue needs unhurried preparation just before serving. So, if you're having more than a few guests, enlist a cohostess to help you with the work.

Since the bread and cheese combination is so filling, follow it up with a simple green salad, a fruit dessert, and beverage.

The popular beef fondue is a bit more elaborate than a cheese fondue, but it is easier on the hostess. Sauces and butters for dipping the cooked meat can be prepared ahead, so that when the party's in progress, you'll need only to keep each guest-chef well supplied with meat. Round out the meal with French bread, salad, and beverage.

Set the tables with colorful table covers and casual tableware, and let the fondue pot do double duty as a centerpiece.

The Shaker-style buffet setting above is simple, utilitarian, and monochromatically striking with stoneware plates and serving dishes, wood-handled flatware tucked in homespun napkins, wood goblets, and a fruit bowl.

In the contemporary version of an old table setting shown above, rich golds and browns predominate in the chunky candleholder, thick bubble goblets, wood-handled flatware, provincial design tablecloth, and stylized plates.

Open House

The open house is a marvelous way to entertain as large a group as you wish — the guest list need be limited only by the size of your home, and your stamina.

This is the occasion when you can mix and match your friends in large numbers. Along with your close friends, invite business associates, your bridge club members and their spouses, the volunteers you work with in your favorite charity, new neighbors, and out-of-town guests.

Stagger the hours of your party, if you expect more than 25 guests. Divide the guest list into two or even three groups. Invite the first group from one to three, the second from two to four, and, if there's a third group, from three to five. By practicing this system, you can comfortably handle a larger guest list without it ever getting too congested. Don't worry if the groups overlap; if guests overstay the departure time, that means they are having a good time and the party's a success.

Almost anything can be served at an open house, but plan your menu well in advance. Some hostesses prefer to serve a mouthwatering array of specially concocted hors d'oeuvres. Others find it just as tempting to serve a menu that consists of a full meal in bite-size proportions. For example, a tray of thinly sliced ham accompanied by rounds of rye bread spread with mustard, a variety of exotic dips and crackers to spread them on, and easy-to-handle desserts such as brownies, and coconut meringues. To be on the safe side, augment your gourmet delicacies with a few old standbys such as crackers and sharp cheeses.

Do all of your food preparation in advance of the party, and if possible, have someone in the kitchen refilling trays.

Assign the beverage service to the host, or if constant beverage service is required, hire someone for the job so the host will be free to circulate among the guests. It is perfectly acceptable to serve guests their first beverage, and then urge them to help themselves to refills.

Plan early where you will set up the serving table. One end of the living room is a logical spot, just as long as it is out of the general flow of traffic. If you have enough room, set the table out from the wall so guests can circulate around it. If the dining room is adjacent to the living room, and large enough for the buffet table, by all means use it. It's a good idea to set up a separate table for beverages.

Don't worry about seating arrangements. Since few guests sit down at this type of party, you may even decide to remove some pieces, or rearrange them, so you have more open space for guests to roam around.

As everyone will be moving from group to group, you should, too. It's your job as hostess not only to greet people as they arrive but to introduce them to others, and see that everyone is enjoying himself.

For the physical comfort of your guests, turn the thermostat down lower than you normally would, keep trafficways clear, and the ventilation good. See that ashtrays are accessible, and emptied often. Your guests will appreciate the attention and consideration—both smokers and nonsmokers. Remove irreplaceable treasures from small tables to avoid accidental breakage.

When the first guests start arriving, have soft, instrumental background music playing. As the number of guests increases and the tempo of the conversation picks up, inconspicuously turn the music off. As the guests thin out, quietly turn on the music again. It's all part of your master plan.

Be sure to use your loveliest tablecloth, an exquisite floral centerpiece, and your liveliest trays and serving pieces to give your buffet table that 'work of art' look.

The dinner for two below features sterling flatware in a traditional pattern in a contemporary setting. Brown plexiglass place mats rest on a gold, orange, and brown striped tablecloth, and gold napkins are in brown napkin rings. The centerpiece repeats same colors.

Your Children's Parties

Children love parties, and in their early years, birthday parties—either their own or those of their friends—are the big social events in their lives. As they grow older, there are many events that can trigger a party—Halloween, scavenger or treasure hunts, skating rink openings, hay rides, or swimming pool, patio, or beach parties.

Some parents go to great expense to engage a clown, a magician, or a puppet show, or even rent a pony for the afternoon for a party for small children. But this is not at all necessary, as a successful party for a child need not strain the budget. Also, children enjoy themselves more when they are actually participating in the activities rather than being a spectator.

Once you've committed yourself to giving a party, go all out and make the party a special event. The ideas need not be new; in fact, tried-and-true favorites are likely to be accepted with great enthusiasm. In all cases, let the children be part of the planning committee. They will know what their age group will enjoy.

If there is doubt as to how many children to invite, the same number as the age of the child is a good guide to follow up until age six. After this, children meet many school friends and may want to invite the entire class. Try to keep the number to a workable eight to ten friends, or your child's party may become an ordeal for you. After age 11, youngsters are apt to prefer pairing off with a few close friends and planning an excursion to a movie or the zoo.

A good time for a party is a Saturday or weekday afternoon for preschoolers, Saturday morning or immediately after school for six and older, or early evening if there's no school the following day for children in the 9-to-11 age group.

It's a good idea to offer to take your party guests home, as this gives you the advantage of controlling the length of the party. It is far better to have a short, happy get-together than a long, drawn out affair. The children will all leave together, and there will be no tired stragglers to contend with after the rest of the group has left.

Although a quick telephone call a day or two in advance of your child's party will suffice, children love receiving and sending mail. Consider having your child design his own invitations or embellish on a pre-created variety. The party may have a special theme—such as cowboys and Indians, come-as-you-are, pirate's treasure, astronauts, etc.—and the invitations should touch off the children's anticipation by reflecting the party theme.

Colorful, casual trimmings will give the party a friendly atmosphere. Expensive, elaborate, or fragile decorations will only make children feel uncomfortable. Balloons are meant to be popped; noisemakers to make noise. Don't expect all the children to behave perfectly—enjoy whatever happens and you'll find children's parties fun to give, even if they may be exhausting. Caution: Remove all of your irreplaceable, fragile treasures to locations that are out of reach during the party hours.

As a rule of thumb, have the refreshments available at the start of the party. If you're serving a meal, always keep it simple and familiar, and be sure not to keep the children waiting too long to eat. It's best to serve the children—especially small-frys—at their accustomed mealtime. Hamburgers, hot dogs, and small sandwiches, along with other finger foods, are ideal for children's parties. Avoid messy meals that require utensils—not to mention concentration.

Instead of serving sweets, tempt children's appetites with dips and vegetable dunkers. 'Childish' his and hers plastic plates, a red and white checked cloth, and a vegetable centerpiece set a happy mood for sailboat sandwiches, crisp vegetables and dip, and mugs of tomato juice with green onion stirrers.

Here's a unique idea for keeping little fingers busy at your next party. Each child's imagination is captured forever on a melamine plate he designs himself—in his favorite colors. These 'small fry originals' come in a kit that contains enough material to make up to 50 drawings. After each guest has created his own

design on this special paper, with the felt tip pens that have nontoxic, quick-drying inks, send the drawings in to be molded into plastic plates. When the plates are delivered a few weeks later, distribute them to each guest as a remembrance of the party. (P.S. Adults will enjoy designing these plates, too.)

If you keep this in mind, clean up will be a snap for you; in addition, you and many a party dress will be spared.

And, don't forget—whatever your menu —to top off the meal with ice cream and cake if the occasion is a birthday celebration. This gives the entire affair a festive note. Remember that to a child, nothing spells out 'Happy Birthday' like a beautifully decorated cake ablaze with candles.

Colorful, unbreakable table settings are perfect for children's parties. Paper plates, cups, and napkins, and plastic dinnerware come in every imaginable color and design. You can mix or match as you wish.

It's a good idea always to have a small-scale stockpile of balloons, a ready-made centerpiece or two, colorful napkins, and party favors. Often, the spur-of-the-moment parties are the most fun for everyone.

Until children are seven or eight, they won't appreciate organized games. Getting them involved in doing and making things together is more likely to result in a happy get-together. Active young children will quickly become bored or restless waiting their turn for pin-the-tail-on-the-donkey or other children's party games.

For a treasure-trove party, a hunt for the key to the 'buried treasure' is the main event of the day. Let each little pirate make his own treasure map; it can also double as a place mat. A gaily decorated treasure chest becomes the centerpiece, and once the key is discovered, the chest is unlocked and small prizes spill out.

All children love to hear a story. Set a party theme around a familiar tale, such as Jack and the Beanstalk. Make Jack's beanstalk centerpiece out of a twisted piece of driftwood with construction paper leaves and beanpods. 'Jack' can be a recycled Christmas pixie or any small doll. An appropriate table covering would be brightly patterned—preferably of spillproof vinyl. Begin by reading the story to the children, and then give them a large bowl of lima beans, some paper, white glue, and colored marking pens. Let the youngsters make whatever character their imaginations produce. Give lots of prizes—for the ugliest, prettiest, most creative, and funniest characters. Soon (and make sure of this), everyone will have won a prize.

Halloween is an excellent occasion for a children's party. Everyone is excited about getting dressed up for 'trick or treat'. For some children, Halloween is the big event of the year. An afternoon party or supper lets them get dressed earlier and start the fun sooner, so the wait for the sun to go down does not seem to be such an eternity. Traditionally, orange and black are the colors of Halloween, but goblins and ghosts come in all colors. There are so many table settings and decorations available for the occasion that it's a rare party-giver that still makes his own. Children can have a great time creating ghouls and witches, but such things as apple bobbing and gaily colored homemade tablecloths and napkins keep the mood happily old-fashioned instead of just scary.

Little touches help give the atmosphere of a full-scale party. A gypsy-caravan table setting may use tambourines, brilliant cloth, basket liners for plates, and a collection of wild grasses in heavy mugs. Mom's skirts and costume jewelry, scarves, and aprons make it fun and easy to look like a band of gypsies. Add appropriate music and props.

If you're looking for a new idea, why not stage a space ship launching party? Have the children come in their own version of spaceman outfits. A robot centerpiece can be fashioned from candy and later devoured. Use tinfoil as a table runner, colorful buttons on a painted box to make a reasonable facsimile of computer for mission control, and serve space food with straws. After judging the costumes, have a relay run in slow motion: last one to the crater wins.

Other child-tested party themes might include an old-fashioned soda shoppe, where the children could concoct their own sundaes; a table draped with fake fur and primitive pottery to greet your African safari; young braves and squaws could gather around a table decked with Navaho-type blanket, Indian corn, beads, and feathers; or maybe a circus or carnival theme would prick their interest and creativity. There is no limit to party themes. In fact, to a youngster, anything is reason enough.

To top off the party on a happy note, pass out baskets of candy and noisemakers on your guests' way out. Allow at least 20 minutes to gather up the crew and their belongings. You'll get them home on time, and their memories will be warm and pleasant.

Cookies in see-through jars grouped around a tabletop Christmas tree, and gaily wrapped packages for a gift exchange provide the table decorations for a children's party. Yellow runners, plates, and mugs add contrast to the deep blue cloth, napkins, and blue-handled flatware. Candy canes add a Christmasy touch.

Etiquette

According to Webster's Dictionary, etiquette is "the forms required by good breeding or prescribed by authority to be observed in social or official life." And, although most people have adopted a more casual life-style in recent years, and much of the formality has gone out of entertaining, there are still some basic rules of etiquette that you should follow.

Guest List

As soon as you decide to entertain, make your guest list. You don't have to invite all your friends every time you have a party. Some people love large, lively cocktail parties, and others prefer small, intimate get-togethers. Invite a group that is compatible and mixes well together.

Invitations

Invitations to informal or semiformal parties can be extended by written invitations, preprinted invitations, or by telephone.

The telephone is the most popular choice today for issuing informal invitations, but be sure to state clearly the date, time, and type of party you are giving.

Acceptances, or regrets, to informal or semiformal parties may be made by phone.

Formal invitations are sent out on various occasions—the formal dinner or dance, the official luncheon or reception and, of course, the wedding and reception. Formal invitations are engraved or handwritten on white or off-white paper, in the third person, and are sent out two weeks ahead.

Acceptances, or regrets, to formal invitations should always be written in the third person, and mailed promptly.

Eating Times

As the hostess, you have a certain amount of leeway when it comes to choosing the time for meals. Although this is a personal preference on your part, it is wise to stay within the limits of local custom. Eating times vary across the country, but most of them stay more or less within the time schedules that are listed below.

Brunch: Between 10:30 a.m. and 1 p.m.
Luncheon: Usually 12:30 or 1 pm.
Buffet luncheon: Usually starts at 12 noon and is served until 2 p.m.
Dinner: Usually 8 p.m. in large metropolitan areas; as early as 6:30 or 7 p.m. in the West and Midwest. If you plan to serve cocktails, invite guests 30 or 45 minutes before dinner time.
Buffet suppers: Usually at 8:30 or 9 p.m. For special occasions, they can be served later, but guests should be so informed.
Coffee parties: Between 10 a.m. and noon.
Tea parties: Usually 4 p.m., but never any later than 4:30 p.m.
Cocktail parties: Usually from 5 to 7 p.m., although personal preference can dictate the hours for the occasion. For instance, when people are working until 5 p.m., hostesses generally prefer to schedule them from 6 to 8 p.m.

Seating Arrangements

Table seating arrangements, which seem to baffle some people, are actually very simple and follow a set pattern.

The seating at a formal luncheon, a formal dinner, and an informal dinner are all the same. The host sits at one end of the table, and the hostess at the opposite end, preferably the end nearest the kitchen. If the honored guest is a male, he is seated on the right of the hostess, and his dinner partner sits at the right of the host. If the honored guest is a woman, it is just the reverse. If there is no guest of honor, the seating is left to your personal preference. Usually, a person of seniority or a guest you see infrequently is placed at the right of the host if it is a woman, or is seated at the right of the hostess if it is a man.

Breakfast

Luncheon

Dinner

Formal Dinner

Table Setting Diagrams

Use the illustrations at the left as a guide to set breakfast, luncheon, and informal and formal dinner tables.

Place the dinnerware and flatware about 1 inch from the edge of the table, and space the settings about 15 inches apart for the comfort and convenience of the diners. Set water glasses or goblets above the point of the knife; wine glasses should go to the right above the spoon.

The breakfast table setting can vary according to the foods served. If the first course is grapefruit, add an extra teaspoon. If no fork foods are included in the menu, omit the fork. If you are serving cereal for breakfast, place the cereal bowl on top of the breakfast plate.

The informal luncheon table setting includes a luncheon plate, bread-and-butter plate, water goblet, six-piece place setting of flatware, and a napkin at the left of the plate. Place the cup and saucer for the beverage on the table when the dessert is served. If you plan to serve a first-course fruit cocktail instead of soup at your informal luncheon, place the teaspoon at the outside. If not, follow the diagram in which it is placed inside for coffee or tea.

For an informal dinner with a traditional menu, use this diagram as your guide. The bread-and-butter plate is optional. If you are not serving a seafood cocktail for the first course, omit the cocktail fork. When serving an appetizer salad first, place the salad fork outside the dinner fork rather than inside as shown. The inside position indicates that the fork is intended for the dessert course.

The formal dinner demands a complete array of flatware, dinnerware, stemware, and an elegant table cover. Do not use a bread-and-butter plate with a formal table setting. Omit the cocktail fork if you are not serving a seafood cocktail. Place the napkin on the service plate instead of at the left, as with other meals. Form a triangle with the water and wine goblets, with the water goblet just above the tips of the knives. When the dessert is served, place the dessert silver on the table.

Limited-Space Dining

How often have you heard someone remark, "I can't entertain guests at meals because I don't have a large enough dining room or dining area —or none at all," or "I never bake for special occasions because I don't have adequate counter space to work on," or "My best tableware is stored away where it's practically impossible to get out when I want it?"

These are all very real problems that confront apartment, condominium, and mobile home dwellers— even those who live in small homes with tiny kitchens, limited dining space, and storage facilities. But these are not insurmountable difficulties, and they should not deter you from serving meals that you enjoy, and from entertaining in style —with table settings that are both attractive and geared to the occasion.

All of these limitations do present a challenge, but with a little advance planning you will find you can prepare everything from hamburgers to gourmet fillet, or from appetizers to a full-course dinner in a small kitchen. And you can serve your culinary efforts with a flourish.

One good way to compensate for a lack of space is to prepare in advance as much of the food as is possible.

You can enhance both the flavor and appearance of the food you serve if you regard the table setting as a basic ingredient. Put your imagination to work, and turn the otherwise routine job of table setting into a creative project. Experiment with different table linens—colorful tablecloths, runners, place mats, and napkins. Mix and match dinnerware, crystal, and flatware, and top it off with an eye-catching centerpiece.

In other words, give just as much consideration to the beauty of your table settings as you would to the inclusion of spices in following a recipe for a main dish casserole.

Putting the 'spice' into your table settings, even though your kitchen and dining space are limited, is what this chapter is all about. You know in advance that it will be more of a task for you than it will be for large home dwellers, but 'forewarned is forearmed,' and it can be done. Put your talents to work, and you'll find that the rewards are many.

← *The casual tableware, chrome and glass table, bamboo wallpaper, natural bamboo chairs, and mesh window shades help to create an airy, spacious feeling for dining in this small area.*

Entertaining in Limited Space

If you have a lot of friends, but not a lot of space in your dining area and kitchen, don't let this stop you from entertaining whenever you are in the mood for sharing food and beverage with others. You may have fallen into the habit of taking your guests out to a restaurant on special occasions, but you've got to admit, there's something so much more hospitable and intimate about entertaining special friends in the privacy of your own home.

If you have qualms about entertaining in what may seem to you to be a much-too-small space, and many people do, you'll soon lose them if you study this section and test some of the space-conquering ideas that are offered. You'll find that there's always room for entertaining graciously if you plan ahead and if you use the facilities you have to the very best advantage.

The appearance of your home, and the atmosphere that prevails in it, can help to create an illusion of spaciousness, or it can make it appear smaller. It's up to you to make a few strategic maneuvers.

You may have a collection of rare and precious objects displayed on small tables that give your home a cozy atmosphere and a personal touch, and this is what you want most of the time. But, when it comes to entertaining, you might like to remove these decorative accessories while the party is in progress. Just leave a few large ashtrays wherever necessary. The same goes for furniture that is arranged to suit your needs. It may be necessary to rearrange a few pieces of furniture that might otherwise obstruct traffic. You can gain still more space if you push the dining table against the wall for a buffet dinner or a cocktail snack service. These tactics will free every inch of available space and allow guests to move about freely.

Because planning is of primary importance when space is at a premium, your imagination and ingenuity are the tools that guarantee success when entertaining.

Once you have decided on your guest list, food, and beverages, put your mind to work on creating an appealing atmosphere.

Decide how you will decorate your table — concoct a novel centerpiece that is in tune with the occasion. Then get out the table linens, dinnerware, flatware, and crystal that you enjoy using. You don't even have to have enough of each pattern for the entire group. Nowadays, it's perfectly acceptable to combine sterling with stainless flatware, and to blend different kinds of china and glassware. Don't be afraid to improvise. When you pool your table setting items, you'll be surprised how lovely your table can be. All of these elements combine to create a mood that counterbalances a lack of space. Everyone appreciates something that has been thoughtfully prepared with tender loving care.

Serving food in a small space is not nearly as difficult as it sounds. The solution is in the choice of foods you will serve — how simply it can be prepared and how easily it can be served and handled. You can save yourself many needless trips in and out of the kitchen if you select food that can be prepared well in advance of your guests' arrival. It's much simpler to choose a main dish that can be cooked in the afternoon and reheated later, or better yet, one that has been prepared days ahead and frozen. Try to avoid dishes that require last-minute attention. Carving, too, can present a problem when you are entertaining in a small space, as can making gravy or mashing potatoes at the last minute.

One-platter meals save room. Place the vegetables around the main dish and garnish with parsley. Another good choice is a main dish casserole or a hearty stew. If you want to eliminate the large salad bowl, place the salad in individual bowls.

Above all, don't be apologetic about your space limitations. If you are relaxed and confident, and enjoying yourself, your guests will also enjoy themselves.

Buffet-Style

There's no doubt that buffet meals are the perfect solution to dining in limited space. Not only can you entertain a larger group than is possible at a sit-down dinner, you'll have fewer problems while serving your guests. In addition, there is a certain informality about a buffet meal that almost everyone likes.

You can set the table anytime during the day, or even the night before. Use a floor-length tablecloth and arrange your plates, napkins, flatware, and crystal. Add a color-coordinated centerpiece and candles to give the table a festive party air.

If your table isn't quite large enough to hold both the table settings and the food, use a buffet server, the top of your desk, or the counter divider between the kitchen and the living room for the food. It is a good idea to use a warming tray or chafing dishes to keep the food hot.

For added convenience, set trays at the end of the table so that guests can use them to carry food back to their chairs. Also, it is more comfortable for them to balance a tray than a small plate.

An even better idea is to buy or borrow some folding tables. Place one next to each guest's chair. Bring out the tables just before dining, and store them right after the meal is finished.

If you are serving wine, fill the glasses and hand one to each guest as he moves away from the table with his plate.

Buffets are informal meals, so here's your chance to add some flair. Use an assortment of serving pieces—ceramic, silver, pewter, crystal, wood, and plastic.

A round table covered with, would you believe, a striped sheet drops one leaf to edge up to the sofa back for a gourmet buffet. Pewter-like plates and pitcher, wood platter, footed wine goblets, glass salad bowl, stainless steel flat-ware, enameled casserole, and yellow saucepan with relishes establish an eclectic look. This is furthered by the centerpiece—a lofty tin watering can filled with yellow irises flanked by chunky candlesticks and candles.

A Family Feast

If you're skeptical about preparing a turkey dinner with all the trimmings in a pint-sized kitchen, and serving it in your dining area, here are some tips on how it can be done. The trick is to take a careful look at your dining strategy.

Take advantage of time-savers—packaged stuffings, instant potatoes, frozen vegetables and pies, canned soups, and cranberry sauce. But, add a few touches of your own to these prepared foods to help produce a meal of traditional elegance.

Plan your cooking schedule carefully, and prepare just as many things as possible ahead of time. This will help you to avoid any last-minute panic.

Set the table ahead, too. Mix and match your favorite dinnerware, crystal, flatware, and table linens to suit the mood of the occasion. And, choose a centerpiece that complements both the food you are serving and the colors of the table setting.

When your guests arrive, serve appetizers and cocktails in the living room. If you mix the cocktails by the pitcher, you will eliminate the confusion that prevails when drinks are individually mixed.

If your dining table is one of the scaled-down versions that are so popular with those who have a small dining area, don't try to place all the food on the table. Serve from a buffet server, a counter divider between the kitchen and the dining area, or a serving cart. Let everyone help themselves, buffet-style. Then, they can all sit down to enjoy the holiday feast.

Sit-Down Dinner

Serving food at a sit-down dinner in a small space requires ingenuity on your part. Dining and drop-leaf tables that are scaled down to fit small dining areas usually can seat four or six comfortably. However, the problem is that once the table is set, there isn't much room left on the table to place the serving dishes.

If you have a buffet server, or a side table with ample surface for hot dishes, this is fine. If you don't have either of these, your best solution is a two- or three-tiered serving cart. After your guests have been seated, wheel out your food-laden cart and place it next to your chair. Pass each dish around for guests to help themselves family-style, then replace the dish on the cart when it returns to you. When the meal is finished, ask the guests to pass their plates to you, and stack them on the bottom tier of the cart. This will clear the table for dessert.

After the dessert course has been served, offer guests their beverage and after-dinner brandy or liqueur in the living room. Place the coffee service on the coffee table. As soon as your guests assemble there, stack the empty serving and dessert plates on the cart and wheel it to the kitchen. It's best to discourage friends from helping you when you're working in crowded conditions. Just clear everything away as quickly and quietly as possible. Leave the tablecloth, candles, and centerpiece on the table until the party is over.

If you don't have a dining table, improvise one by placing a large piece of plywood on top of two saw horses. Cover it with a floor-length cloth, and no one will be the wiser. Or, buy a large, round plywood tabletop and three screw-in legs. Cover it with a floor-length table cover, and use folding metal or wooden garden chairs.

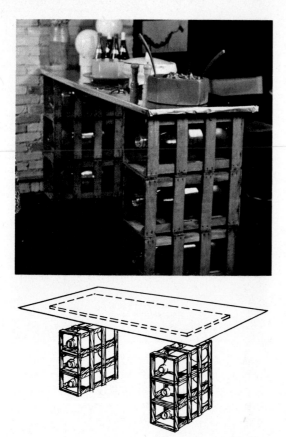

Bottle Bar

When your friends drop by for cocktails, serve them from a unique homemade 'bottle bar.' You may have to search around a bit to find large-size commercial bottles, one each in a crate, but the rewards will be worth your while. Stack up the crates, three at either end, and top them with a rectangular piece of ¾-inch plywood covered with Mylar. You can't beat this unusual idea for an easy way to achieve an instant beverage center for your entertaining needs.

Shuttered Buffet Server

If you are in dire need of an attractive, functional server for buffet meals, why not build the shuttered buffet server that is pictured below? It's easy to make, and it requires only a few hand tools.

Materials include four 12x32-inch unfinished shutters, plastic laminate, 2-inch pine lumber, ¾-inch plywood, and 1x2s. Cut the ¾-inch plywood into a 22x78-inch top, and band it with 1x2s. Apply plastic laminate to the top, or substitute colorful adhesive-backed vinyl. Install the shutters and 22-inch-square glued-up shelves with metal brackets. Paint or stain the server to achieve the finish of your choice.

What could be more appropriate for informal dining than the 'bottle bar' above. By placing it near the kitchen, you can use it for an instant beverage center, and for serving food. Instructions for making it are at the right.

← *The reflective qualities of the see-through glass tabletop, chrome base, and chair frame tend to expand the dining space visually. The bowl of oranges, candles and candleholders, napkins, and place mats pick up the orange in the geometric-patterned wallpaper.*

The informal shutter buffet server at the right → *can take its place indoors, on the porch, or on the patio. It is easy to build, and you will find it indispensable for informal entertaining occasions. There are instructions at the right to explain how to build it.*

The melamine dinnerware above, being contemporary in design, harmonizes well with the textured handwoven runner, the chunky crystal goblet, vase, and the candleholders. This dinnerware is exceedingly durable, dishwasher safe, and stackable, so the entire set requires only a minimum of storage space. This innovative design represents a new concept in dinnerware, and the bright colors add a happy note to any meal—either indoors or on the patio.

Luncheons

The midday luncheon is usually given during the week, and more often than not, it's a ladies-only get-together. As such, this is a perfect occasion for introducing new acquaintances to old friends, for honoring an out-of-town guest, to organize a charitable project, or just to chat with friends.

Luncheons today are not the formal occasions they once were. The many-course luncheon of the past has given way to a much lighter meal. It may consist only of a main course, a beverage, and a dessert. If the luncheon is for women only, the menu can be dainty and even a little bit fancy. If men are invited to the luncheon, make the courses hardy. In almost every group there are a few people who are diet-conscious, especially at lunchtime. In deference to them, avoid serving high-calorie foods.

Decorate your table with cheerful colors— a floral, plaid, striped, or solid color tablecloth or place mats, and matching napkins. Center the table with a low container of flowers in matching hues. Use your best dinnerware, flatware, and crystal. And remember to keep the table uncluttered for a pleasing effect.

As with other types of limited-space dining, prepare the food and set the table as much as possible in advance. If your table is too small to hold everything, set the food out buffet-style. Or, you can set the food on a buffet or serving cart close to you and serve it family-style.

Cocktails before a luncheon are optional. If you do serve them, be sure to include some light beverages and some non-alcoholic ones. While your guests are enjoying their beverages, you can complete your last-minute food preparations in the kitchen.

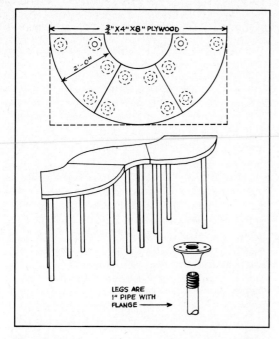

The three-part serpentine serving table above is simple to make, and it is inexpensive. For the tabletop you will need a 4x8-foot panel of ¾-inch plywood. Cut it according to the diagram above. Make the leg sections of 1-inch

pipe, and fasten them to each section of the top. Cover the three tabletops with metallic Mylar. You can use these tables individually, or you can form them into a 'U' or 'S' shape, depending on your entertaining needs.

Brunches

Brunches and luncheons are alike in that they're both scheduled at about the same time of day, but there the similarity ends.

The brunch usually is held on a weekend or holiday around noon. This makes it a popular means of entertaining for the working homemaker. If your brunch is to be on a Sunday morning, set the time so that it is convenient for church-going guests.

A brunch can be as simple or as lavish as you wish. You may decide on the spur-of-the-moment to invite a few friends to an informal brunch, or you may spend weeks planning an elegant smorgasbord-type brunch. Regardless of the formality, this is an occasion when you can be as flamboyant as you wish with your table settings. Casual dinnerware and colorful tablecloths or place mats and napkins will set a happy mood.

Usually, brunch menus feature a fruit or fruit juice, hot breads or toast, assorted marmalades and jellies, a meat or meat casserole main dish, and eggs. Coffee, tea, or hot chocolate are the standard beverages. If you start with alcoholic beverages, serve bloody marys or screwdrivers.

To allow yourself more time to visit with your guests, make use of warming trays, chafing dishes, and electric or insulated serving dishes. These items will keep your food temptingly hot for guests who come back for seconds. It's also a good idea to choose a main dish that can be prepared well in advance of guest arrivals, and you can rest assured that the food will stay hot.

If you have invited more guests than you can seat comfortably at your dining table, let each guest use a tray or a folding tray table. That way, no one has to balance a plate on his lap (men especially hate this).

The Single Homemaker

When you have to be groomed and dressed for a party, greet guests at the door as they arrive, prepare and serve food and beverages, take part in the conversation and enjoy yourself, and finally do the clean-up chores afterward, there has to be a work simplification program in progress.

The key to successful entertaining by the single homemaker is organization and timing. You can manage all this—without a caterer or a crisis—if you plan ahead.

Do your grocery and beverage shopping days ahead of time. Be sure to take a list with you so you don't have to make a mad dash to the store at the last minute.

Serve simple fare—a hearty stew, a seafood casserole, or a fondue. These can fall into the 'meal fit for a king' category if you follow a tried-and-true recipe. Then, embellish it with a tray of relishes, a tempting salad with a surprise dressing, bread or rolls, beverage, and a make-ahead dessert. Spare yourself the last-minute panic of coping with canapés. Instead, serve a cheese ball or dip and let guests make their own hors d'oeuvres, tiny meatballs, or cocktail wieners in a tasty sauce.

Whether you are planning a sit-down or buffet meal, or a tea or cocktail party, decide what table settings you will use, and get them out the night before and set the table. Experiment with different arrangements to see which one will be the most attractive and the most functional.

Plan your centerpiece well ahead of time, too. If you decide to order flowers, be sure to give your florist explicit information as to your color scheme, the mood you are trying to create, and the size of arrangement that will be most suitable. If you are arranging your own floral centerpiece, do it several hours before the guests are due to

Single homemakers, particularly, will enjoy ovenproof dinnerware such as the earthenware below, with its green, blue, and brown tones. When you use oven-to-table serving pieces, *you don't have to transfer food from cookware to serving dishes. This reduces clutter in the kitchen, cuts down serving time, and allows you to spend more time with your guests.*

This setting is ideal for the bachelor who likes spur-of-the-moment entertaining. The paper plates, napkins, and place mats, plus the plastic cocktail glasses and flatware, are a coordi- *nated grouping that can be disposed of quickly when the guests are gone. Serve a main dish casserole, a salad, bread or rolls, and a beverage, and you're all set.*

arrive. If you want to make a non-floral centerpiece, dream up your creation several days ahead of time.

If you serve punch from a punch bowl, or cocktails from a pitcher, you can eliminate confusion in the kitchen. Or, if you do serve cocktails individually mixed, set up a temporary bar in the living room. Use large trays to hold all the equipment so there won't be any damage from accidental spillage. Except for the ice, all bar equipment can be set up hours before the party. Ask one of the early arrivals to serve cocktails.

Small kitchens are not conducive to the offers of volunteer K.P. help. Oftentimes, an extra person in the kitchen only makes it more congested. It's much better to plan

a simple menu of food that you can fix ahead of time, thereby keeping last-minute preparations to a minimum.

A serving cart is a real blessing for the single homemaker, especially for bachelors who entertain frequently and pride themselves on doing it with the utmost of ease. Use the serving cart for beverage, dessert, and after-dinner brandies. When you sit down at the table with your guests, the table is set for the main course. Keep the serving cart at your side, and you won't have a single trip to the kitchen until after the meal is finished.

After a successful party, even cleanup chores aren't so dismal. One of your guests may even offer to stay and help.

Pots of parsley, chive, dill, and marjoram are a perfect centerpiece for a soup party. A metal salad bowl serves as the soup container, with footed cups for individual servings.

Use a punch bowl to serve fruit soup, and punch cups for individual servings. You can use a punch bowl for any cold soups. The centerpiece is an arrangement of dried dillweed.

Soup's On

Hot and hearty soup served with a flourish is ideal for cold-weather entertaining. It's especially appropriate for the single host or hostess, as most of the preparations can be done in advance.

You can create your own masterpiece from scratch—examine your cookbooks for interesting possibilities. Or, you can experiment with prepared soup mixes.

Even if you don't own a handsome soup tureen, you can still serve soup. There are many other pieces of dinnerware and cookware that can double as a soup dispenser. You'll notice that there's not a single tureen in the pictures on this page.

Even though the soup is the main attraction, don't neglect the rest of the table. Whether you plan to serve your guests sit-down-style or buffet-style, be sure to arrange appetizers, relishes, and tidbits in an

Use a coffee server as a soup dispenser for any kind of soup that pours easily, and metal cups instead of soup bowls. Make a topiary tidbit container out of three woven baskets.

You can please all your guests by offering a choice of hot or chilled soup. Serve them from heat-resistant kitchen canisters. Two polar bear figurines double as a centerpiece.

attractive manner, and create some novel type of centerpiece that is compatible with the food and the occasion.

This type of entertaining is perfect for those occasions when you want to invite your friends over after a football game or an evening at the theater. You'll find that these 'souped up' settings will satisfy even those with ravenous appetites.

Serving Meals in Your Kitchen

If you have an eating area in your kitchen, or a built-in breakfast bar, you can entertain a few guests there. Kitchens have long been referred to as the heart of the home, and historically they have been noted for their spirit of warmth and hospitality. Even today, they are the gathering places for families and friends.

Meals that are best served in the kitchen are breakfasts, brunches, and late-evening snacks. Even though the setting is casual, the meals will be remembered with pleasure if you plan them carefully.

Always plan a menu that can be prepared well in advance. This way, your sink and kitchen counters won't be cluttered with pots, pans, and mixing bowls. Even if you do have some foods to prepare at the last minute, try to wash and put away all of the utensils you use before your guests sit down. Also, this is an especially good time to use colorful oven-to-table casseroles and skillets. Another tip for adding much-needed work space is to tuck away any small appliances that you won't be using for this particular meal—toaster, blender, broiler, frypans, skillets.

When you're entertaining in the kitchen, be just as selective about your table settings as you would be if you were planning a formal sit-down meal in the dining room. This is your chance to let your creative impulses run wild. For example, use colorful handwoven place mats, matching napkins in wood napkin rings, stoneware or earthenware dinnerware, heavy water goblets and wine goblets (if you are serving wine), and stainless flatware. Mix or match your tableware to set the mood. Be sure to allow room for a centerpiece. If you have flowers, that's fine; if you don't, look around for something that is equally attractive. Even relishes, if they are artistically arranged, easily can double as a centerpiece.

Sharing a Sunday morning breakfast with a friend is a good way to start a new week. It's even fun to eat it in the kitchen when the table is set with handcrafted dinnerware and a bas- *ket centerpiece filled with dried material. The table isn't cluttered with serving pieces, toaster, or broiler because they can stay on the kitchen counter and still be convenient for serving.*

Caring for Tableware

The splendid collection of tableware that produces 'oohs' and 'ahs' from your friends and relatives will last a lifetime if you store and care for it properly.

Entertaining should be a happy experience—with a pleasing atmosphere, a dining table set with care and imagination, good food that fits the mood you are striving for, and stimulating conversation with your friends and family. This spirit of conviviality can be lessened drastically, however, if there is a series of minor aggravations just because the tableware is not easily accessible and ready to be used by you whenever the occasion arises.

There's nothing more frustrating than to have your best set of dinnerware tucked away on the top shelf of a cabinet where it is almost inaccessible. Balancing yourself on a wobbly kitchen stool or small ladder while you are lifting it down from the cabinet is a hazardous experience in itself. Then, after you do get it down, more than likely you'll find that it has collected a film of dust, which means that a dishwashing job is imperative. By this time, your pride in your cherished possessions drops to an all-time low. Add to this the fact that you have to replace the china in the same hard-to-reach storage space after the party is over and the dishwashing chores are done, and the situation appears even gloomier.

Although not everyone has an ample amount of storage space that allows them to have a punch bowl, serving trays, or a fondue pot within easy reach, with a little planning and organization you can arrange tableware so that it is stored in a manner that best fits your needs. Store tableware that you use most often in the most convenient location. Relegate those items that you seldom use to less handy storage areas. Also, it can be a real time-saver to keep a list of seldom-used items telling where they are stored.

When budgeting your time for homemaking chores, allow time on a regular basis for planning and reorganizing the storage of your dinnerware so that it is always in the most convenient location. At the same time you are reorganizing, wash everything before you store it again.

The same applies to flatware. Much of the fun of entertaining is gone if you have to do a rush job of cleaning and polishing the flatware shortly before guests arrive. You may even do less entertaining than you would like to do just because of the tedious last-minute chores involved.

These same problems are not likely to be incurred with the tableware you use daily because the frequent washing of dinnerware keeps it dust-free, and also keeps the silverware tarnish-free.

In most cases, the investment you place in dinnerware, flatware, stemware and glassware, and table linens is a substantial one. So, protect your investment with great care. You will undoubtedly use many of these items most of your life, even though you add to your collection as the years go by. So that your tableware will maintain its lovely appearance for many years to come, avail yourself of all the information possible on how to care for it.

On the next few pages you will find a wide variety of helpful suggestions for maintaining your tableware. Put these ideas into practice. You will be amazed at how even the simplest fare will take on a gourmet touch if your tableware presents a well-cared-for appearance.

Storing Tableware

Whether you have only a modest supply or a large collection of tableware, there are still storage problems. You can minimize or even eliminate these problems and get more enjoyment from your tableware if you do a little planning and organizing.

How to Store Dinnerware

Fine china is amazingly durable, but when you are storing it, do be sure to use separating pads between the plates. If you don't have the pads, use paper napkins. For fine china that you use infrequently, it is best to store it in zippered, quilted cases of padded plastic with protector pads. These will protect dinnerware from both dust and breakage. Never stack the cups. Place them individually on shelves or hang them on hooks or on cup racks.

Stack glass, ceramic, plastic, earthenware, and ironstone dinnerware one on top of another with no pads between each one—without fear of damaging them. But don't slide one onto another; place them one at a time on top of another.

If your storage space is at a premium, cabinet organizers are the perfect solution. Dinnerware racks that hold a service for eight in a minimum of space, cup stackers, revolving or sliding cup racks, place racks, and platter racks that are made from welded steel frames covered with a cushion-coating will protect your dinnerware from nicks, knocks, and accidental breakage.

How to Store Flatware

When you are not using your flatware daily, keep it in a closed drawer, away from the tarnishing elements that are present in the air—especially smoke.

If you have a buffet, hutch cabinet, chest, or small table with a tarnishproof lined drawer, you can have easy access to your silverware. At the same time, you can keep it bright and shiny.

If you don't have one or more tarnishproof lined drawers, store your flatware in tarnishproof flannel cases.

How to Store Hollow Ware

Store hollow ware—silver trays, candlesticks, and serving dishes—in either tarnishproof flannel cases or in polyethylene bags to retard tarnish. If you don't use your hollow ware pieces frequently, put some gum camphor in the bag to keep out the moisture. Never close these bags with a piece of elastic or a rubber band, as rubber permanently defaces silver. Instead, use a piece of string or cord.

How to Store Glassware

Always store your crystal right side up on shelves to avoid chipping the drinking edge, and allow space between each piece. If you do find any small nicks, gently file the rough edge with 00 emery paper wrapped around a blunt tool. This will result in a frosted edge, which you can touch up with polishing rouge on a leather strap. Rub gently in both operations.

How to Store Table Linens

Store table linens away from any areas where there is excessive heat. Air out and refold every six months those table linens that you don't use often. If possible, roll all the tablecloths and table runners on cardboard mailing tubes after ironing to eliminate creases, and store them in long drawers or deep linen closets.

You can add a spicy fragrance to your storage drawers by placing an old-fashioned pomander or 'clove orange' in each one.

For place mats, plenty of shallow sliding trays and drawers are ideal. Never roll place mats—rolling fabric place mats tends to wrinkle them; rolling synthetic place mats results in breaking the fibers.

Special Care Tips

Tableware, like everything else you have in your home, can become shabby with use. But if you clean it with reasonable care, you can prolong its life and good looks.

How to Wash Dinnerware

Although accidental breakage and chipping present the first challenge in caring for your dinnerware, a few simple washing instructions will help to eliminate abrasions and cuts in the glaze. They will also help to keep it sparkling clean.

Here are the washing instructions for the four common types of dinnerware.

Fine china can be washed either in a dishwasher or by hand. In either case, rinse it as soon as possible after use, and don't let coffee dry in cups. If coffee or tea has dried in the cups, use borax on a soft cloth to remove stains. Never use an abrasive cleaning powder. Also, never scrape remains of food off plates—use a paper napkin or rinse them off.

If you're washing fine china by hand, use a rubber mat in the bottom of the sink and a nozzle on the tap. Use whatever soap or detergent you prefer, and wash with a soft brush or wiper. Never use steel wool or soap pads when washing fine china, and be sure to remove your diamond rings. A diamond will scratch almost any surface, leaving a scar. Rinse dishes in hot water, and air-dry them upright in a plastic- or rubber-coated dish rack.

Fine china can be washed in an automatic dishwasher, too, but certain precautions must be taken. Be sure that your plates are properly loaded so that they don't rub against one another and cause scratching. Also, select a mild soap or detergent that carries the stamp of approval of the American Fine China Guild.

Ceramic, earthenware, or ironstone dinnerware should be washed in the same manner as fine china. Some hand-painted dinnerware that has been improperly fired will not withstand any kind of vigorous washing. If you are in doubt about any particular type of dinnerware, follow the manufacturer's directions. Many brands come with washing instructions included.

Glass-ceramic dinnerware is completely dishwasher-safe—even the patterns with metallic bandings. Detergents won't harm the finish and decorations won't wash off. This type of dinnerware needs no special care regardless of whether it is washed by hand or in a dishwasher.

Plastic dishes can be washed safely in a dishwasher. These dishes have colors and patterns molded right into the pieces that can't fade or wear off. Just don't scrub the surface with cleaning pads or any type of gritty cleanser.

Washing/Cleaning Flatware

All flatware should be washed, rinsed in hot water, and dried quickly after use in order to retain its luster. The amount of care that is needed to preserve the beauty of your flatware depends primarily on the metal you select.

Sterling silver requires the most care, but if you use it frequently—every day if you wish—it will need polishing less often. If you have a large service and use it for only two or three people, rotate the pieces so each piece is used and washed every few days. Wash or rinse the silver as soon as possible after meals, as numerous foods cause tarnish when the silver remains unwashed for a period of time.

If you wash your sterling silver by hand, don't overload the dishpan. All types of metals are susceptible to scratches, and in most cases, this is the result of crowding the pieces. Don't be discouraged if you notice some fine scratches on your sterling. These are most conspicuous when the silver is new. Eventually, polishing will blend them so the luster, or patina, resembles that of old silver.

Choose a good silver polish, and use lengthwise, never circular, strokes when you are using it. Keep your sterling away from salt and anything made of rubber. Either one can permanently deface silver.

Silverplated flatware has an outer surface of silver, so it requires the same treatment you give fine sterling.

Gold electroplated flatware needs no special handling. It is highly resistant to both wear and tarnish, and it can be washed safely in a dishwasher. The precious gold plating is applied in a manner that makes it extremely durable.

Stainless flatware is the easiest type to care for. It is dishwasher safe and does not tarnish. However, discoloration can occur. This can be from a gradual buildup of some foods, from some detergents, or from the chemical action that occurs when stainless is washed with a cleaning agent in an aluminum pan. This discoloration can be removed easily with stainless or copper polish. It is less apt to occur if you use a plastic dishpan when washing it.

How to Care for Glassware

To keep your stemware and glassware glistening, use mild suds and warm water for washing. Never use caustic powders. A few drops of bluing or ammonia in the dishwater will add luster. Rinse in cool water, drain, and dry with lint-free towel. Polish gently with the towel, but don't squeeze your whole fist inside glassware.

Be sure to place a rubber mat in the bottom of the sink, and place a folded tea towel on the drainboard. It's a good idea to rinse delicate stemware in a plastic dishpan, as it's very easy to chip it against the spout if you hold it directly under the running water to rinse it.

Avoid sudden temperature changes. Extreme heat causes glass to expand; extreme cold causes it to contract. Both can result in cracking. Never pour boiling water over glasses, especially stemware, and don't put ice water in a glass that is still hot from washing. Always put a silver spoon in a glass cup before filling it with hot liquid to prevent it from cracking.

How to Care for Table Linens

Laundering table linens is not the time-consuming task that it once was because of the many permanent press fabrics now available. If your table linens have this easy-care built-in feature, follow the manufacturer's laundering instructions.

If they don't, use warm suds and several rinses of clear water to ensure removal of dirt and detergents. Water temperature should be between 100 and 110 degrees for rayons, colored cottons, and linens.

After the linens are washed and dried, sprinkle and iron them. Be sure to refer to the hang tags for fiber content and any special instructions that are recommended.

Fold tablecloths down the center, but don't crease this fold with the iron, just lightly fold the cloth over. Each time you launder the cloth, move the fold a little to the right or left of the center to keep it from wearing out in one spot.

Iron monogrammed or embroidered table linens on a thickly padded board or a thick turkish towel. Press the wrong side first to bring out the design.

Helpful Hints

• If table linens need mending, do this before laundering, as the washing may accentuate frayed areas and holes. Also, remove any spots before laundering.

• If you have inadvertently stacked glasses one inside another, and they become stuck, do not pry them apart. Fill the inside glass with cold water, and immerse the outer one in warm water.

• If you add ammonia or bluing to water to add luster to glassware, wash metallic-banded glassware separately—by hand.

• Use a small, soft brush for cleaning the crevices in ornamental silver.

• Fine china should be warmed gradually; never place it in a hot oven.

INDEX

Acknowledgments

We are happy to acknowledge our indebtedness and to express our sincere thanks to the following who have been helpful to us in producing this book:

Alderman Studios
Carnival Creations, Inc.
Heller Designs Inc.
Joanna Western Mills
Oneida Ltd. Silversmiths
Party House Inc.
C. D. Peacock
Poppytrail Div., Metlox
Potteries
Royal Worcester
Teleflora
Texasware Div., Plastics
Mfg. Co.
The Gorham Company
The Jack Denst Designs, Inc.
Vernonware Div., Metlox
Potteries
Jan De Bard
David Harrison
Fae Huttenlocher
Herb Mitchell
Eulalah Overmeyer
Gordon Schmultz
Buddy Waldrop
Jack Wozniak